BUS

# INTEGRATING ISO 14001 INTO A QUALITY MANAGEMENT SYSTEM

Also available from ASQ Quality Press

*Implementing ISO 14001*
Marilyn R. Block

*The ISO 14000 Handbook*
Joseph Cascio, editor

*ISO 14000: Questions and Answers, Fourth Edition*
Mark Baker and Mary McKiel

*Quality, Safety, and Environment: Synergy in the 21st Century*
Pascal Dennis

*The Quality Audit Handbook*
ASQ Quality Audit Division, J.P. Russell, editing director

*Nimble Documentation: The Practical Guide for World-Class Organizations*
Adrienne Escoe

To request a complimentary catalog of publications,
call 800-248-1946.

# INTEGRATING ISO 14001 INTO A QUALITY MANAGEMENT SYSTEM

Marilyn R. Block

I. Robert Marash

ASQ Quality Press
Milwaukee, Wisconsin

Block, Marilyn R.
    Integrating ISO 14001 into a quality management system/Marilyn
R. Block, I. Robert Marash.
    p.   cm.
    Includes index.
    ISBN 0-87389-399-9 (alk. paper)
        1. ISO 14000 Series Standards.   2. ISO 9001.   3. Quality control.
    I. Marsh, I. Robert, 1943–   . II. Title.
TS155.7.B57  1999
658.5'62--dc21                                                      98-52672
                                                                        CIP

10 9 8 7 6 5 4 3
ISBN 0-87389-399-9

Acquisitions Editor: Ken Zielske
Project Editor: Annemieke Koudstaal
Production Coordinator: Shawn Dohogne

ASQ Mission: The American Society for Quality advances individual and
organizational performance excellence worldwide by providing opportunities for learning, quality improvement, and knowledge exchange.

Attention: Bookstores, Wholesalers, Schools and Corporations:
ASQ Quality Press books, videotapes, audiotapes, and software are available at quantity discounts with bulk purchases for business, educational, or
instructional use. For information, please contact ASQ Quality Press at
800-248-1946, or write to ASQ Quality Press, P.O. Box 3005, Milwaukee,
WI 53201-3005.

To place orders or to request a free copy of the ASQ Quality Press Publications Catalog, including ASQ membership information, call 800-248-1946.
Visit our web site at http://www.asq.org.

Printed in the United States of America

  Printed on acid-free paper

**American Society for Quality**

Quality Press
611 East Wisconsin Avenue
Milwaukee, Wisconsin 53202
Call toll free 800-248-1946
www.asq.org
http://qualitypress.asq.org
http://standardsgroup.asq.org
http://e-standards.asq.org
E-mail: authors@asq.org

For Joel

and

Barbara, Alexander, and Meredith

Let's read this together!

# TABLE OF CONTENTS

# LIST OF FIGURES

# Introduction

This book takes two topics—quality management systems and environmental management systems—that have received extensive treatment as stand-alone systems and presents information that will enable organizations to integrate the requirements imposed by two distinct standards into one cohesive management system. This effort is based on the following assumptions.

- Companies pursuing integration have a mature quality management system in place and will expand that system to accommodate ISO 14001.
- The existing quality management system conforms to ISO 9001, ISO 9002, or QS-9000.

Integration can occur in two ways. Full integration results in a single system that addresses all requirements imposed by ISO 14001 and the guiding quality management standard. As a result, all system-related activities are designed without differentiation between "quality" and "environmental" concerns. There is one systems manual, one set of procedures, one audit that looks at combined requirements, and one management review.

Partial integration is the approach taken by companies that want to keep separate their quality management and environmental management system internal audit review processes, as well as registration audits and surveillance audits. Two system manuals are developed—one for the quality management system and one for the environmental management system.

Where appropriate, the environmental management system uses procedures from the quality management system. When such procedures must be modified to fulfill ISO 14001 requirements, a company has the flexibility to modify them only as they pertain to the environmental management system, thereby ensuring that the quality management system is not compromised. One outcome of this approach is two sets of documentation, much of which may be redundant.

One of the primary advantages of integration is the need to bring together quality assurance and environmental staff. In our work with ISO 9000-registered companies that want to implement ISO 14001, the authors have witnessed numerous examples where quality assurance staff were woefully ignorant about the company's environmental impacts and legal obligations and environmental staff were unaware of established procedures related to document control, records, and other similar activities. The book is organized into nine chapters that enable the reader to move directly to issues of particular interest.

Chapter 1, The Decision to Integrate Quality Management and Environmental Management Systems, discusses the purpose of quality management and environmental management systems, differentiates between partial and full integration of such systems, and addresses the benefits of integration.

Chapter 2, Quality Management and Environmental Management System Standard Similarities, describes both the similarities and differences between ISO 9001/2 and ISO 14001. The explicit requirements contained in each standard are reviewed in order to delineate those requirements with direct overlap, those with partial overlap, and those that are unique.

Chapter 3, Getting Started, delineates specific activities essential to the evaluation of the existing quality system and documentation and implementation of an integrated system. It describes how to assess existing quality procedures and established practices through gap analysis in order to minimize the documentation requirements imposed by an integrated system. This chapter also provides guidance on estimating the amount of time needed to effectively complete all identified activities.

Chapter 4, Documenting the Integrated Management System, focuses on the four levels of documents employed in the design and implementation of quality management and environmental management systems.

Chapter 5, Combined Procedures, identifies the differences in documentation requirements. ISO 9001/2 requires that all system-level procedures be documented, while ISO 14001 mandates documentation for only two such procedures. The chapter also discusses how an organization can most effectively articulate required procedures.

Chapter 6, Internal System Audits, addresses the requirement imposed by both ISO 9001/2 and ISO 14001 that the organization periodically audit the system to verify its conformance to standard requirements. The chapter discusses how internal audits should be conducted and what special considerations must be brought to bear when auditing an integrated system.

Chapter 7, Management Review, compares the purpose of quality management and environmental management system reviews. The challenges inherent in review of an integrated system are delineated. Methods of documentation and follow-up actions in response to review findings are presented.

Chapter 8, The Registration Audit, discusses the advantages and disadvantages of obtaining registration for an integrated system versus separate quality management and environmental management system registrations. The typical audit experience—preassesment, desktop review and conformity assessment, and corrective action plan—is described.

Chapter 9, Conclusion, addresses ISO efforts to achieve compatibility between ISO 9001/2 and ISO 14001. Elements of the proposed ISO 9001 revision (to be published in 2000) are compared to those in ISO 14001.

Appendix A contains the quality manual developed by an ISO 9002-registered company (renamed here as Mega Manufacturing). Appendix B presents the same manual after revision to integrate ISO 14001 requirements.

The acronym ISO refers to the International Organization for Standardization in Geneva, Switzerland. All references in this book to ISO 9001, ISO 9002, QS-9000 and ISO 14001 pertain to the following standards.

ISO 9001    ANSI/ISO/ASQC Q9001-1994, Quality Systems—
            Model for Quality Assurance in Design, Development,
            Production, Installation, and Servicing

ISO 9002     ANSI/ISO/ASQC Q9002-1994, Quality Systems—
Model for Quality Assurance in Production,
Installation, and Servicing

QS-9000     Quality System Requirements QS-9000, second
edition, Automotive Industry Action Group,
Southfield, Michigan

ISO 14001    ANSI/ISO 14001-1996, Environmental Management
Systems—Specifications with Guidance for Use

# CHAPTER 1

## The Decision to Integrate Quality Management and Environmental Management Systems

The majority of organizations interested in implementing an environmental management system (EMS) that conforms to ISO 14001 are registered to ISO 9001, ISO 9002, or QS-9000. This may reflect greater concern with quality in all facets of internal management or familiarity with and acceptance of ISO standards as a management framework. Regardless, such companies want to implement an EMS that builds upon the foundation provided by their quality management systems.

The authors' experience in implementing ISO 14001 since it was published in September, 1996, has demonstrated that integrating an EMS into an existing quality management system (QMS) is far less costly, time-consuming, and difficult than creating a stand-alone system.

Integration can be accomplished in two ways—partial integration or full integration. A partially integrated quality management and environmental management system keeps separate the quality manual and EMS manual. However, instead of creating a completely separate set of system-level procedures, the EMS utilizes those quality procedures that are easily applied to environmental issues, for example, document control. An effective document control procedure is as applicable to documents required by the EMS as to those required by the quality management system for which it was developed.

In a partially integrated system, QMS procedures with some similarity can be modified and enhanced for the EMS. Assignment of unique EMS document numbers ensures that modifications apply only to the EMS, thereby leaving the quality procedure unchanged for quality management purposes and avoiding problems at future surveillance or reregistration audits.

A fully integrated system contains one manual that addresses the combined QMS and EMS requirements. Existing QMS procedures are modified to capture the specific elements mandated by each governing standard.

One of the most important questions facing companies with registered quality management systems that want to implement an EMS is whether to partially or fully integrate the two. Neither choice is inherently better than the other. Organizational structure, management style, and scope of the system will influence which approach is preferable.

- Organizational structure—In a centralized organization, a core group of decision makers determines how all functional units within the organization are to conduct business. Such organizations are more likely to favor fully integrated systems, which typically are developed at the corporate level and distributed to business units for implementation.

  In a decentralized organization, individual business units make their own decisions about how they will operate. Because individual business units develop their own systems, often without assistance from corporate staff or other business units, they tend to favor partially integrated systems which are easier to document.

- Management style—Autocratic organizations typically favor partially integrated systems. This most likely reflects a desire to rigidly compartmentalize activities such that the QMS is the purview of the quality department and the EMS is the responsibility of the environmental department. Participatory organizations tend to be more amenable to implementing fully integrated systems, which require cross-functional teams to be effective.

- Scope—Fully integrated systems are more common in organizations where the EMS is intended to apply to the same business unit or product line as the quality management system. Organizations in which the scope of the EMS differs somewhat from that of the QMS often find it easier to implement a partially integrated system.

These factors are summarized in Figure 1.1.

| Corporate Culture | Full Integration | Partial Integration |
|---|---|---|
| Organizational Structure | Centralized | Decentralized |
| Management Style | Participatory | Autocratic |
| Scope of System | EMS applied to same business or product as QMS | EMS applied to different business or product than QMS |

**Figure 1.1**   Factors Influencing Full versus Partial Integration

Ultimately, the decision to fully or partially integrate the quality management and environmental management systems should hinge on what makes the most sense from an internal management perspective. The system must be designed in a manner that ensures employee understanding, leverages previous successes, and streamlines management decisions.

## INTENT OF A QUALITY MANAGEMENT SYSTEM

The intent of ISO 9001 and ISO 9002 is twofold. These standards provide both a framework for companies that want to implement effective quality management systems and requirements against which companies can evaluate the quality management systems of their suppliers. ISO 9001, ISO 9002, and the auto industry standard, QS-9000, are used by suppliers to fulfill quality management requirements imposed by their customers.

## INTENT OF AN ENVIRONMENTAL MANAGEMENT SYSTEM

Unlike a quality management system (QMS) that assures customers that their order requirements will be met consistently, an environmental management system (EMS) focuses on improving a company's environmental performance through prevention of pollution efforts. Related benefits are cost savings and improved relations with state environmental agencies.

### Improved Environmental Performance

Although ISO 14001 is not an environmental performance standard, its authors intended that the implementation of an EMS will result in improved environmental performance. This expectation is embodied in three explicit requirements.

- Articulation of an environmental policy—ISO 14001 stipulates that the policy must be appropriate to a company's environmental impacts, commit to prevention of pollution, and provide the framework for developing objectives and targets.
- Identification of significant environmental impacts—Every element of a company's activities that can interact with the environment must be identified and evaluated to determine whether it causes a detrimental or beneficial change to the environment.
- Delineation of objectives and targets—Objectives and targets must be consistent with a company's environmental policy; therefore, prevention of pollution must be emphasized.

These requirements, which form the foundation upon which a company's EMS is built, ensure that implementation of an EMS will improve environmental performance.

### Reduced Costs

The ISO 14001 emphasis on prevention of pollution can reduce costs in two ways. First, expenditures on raw materials may decrease. Second, costs related to the treatment, transport, and disposal of concomitant waste streams are reduced.

Evaluation of environmental impacts frequently uncovers opportunities to reduce or replace hazardous materials. A reduction in the amount of material purchased results in lower costs both for initial purchase and for end-of-pipe activities related to waste streams. Elimination of hazardous materials and replacement with more benign substances is not necessarily cheaper (the replacement material may be more expensive than its predecessor) but total costs may be reduced because end-of-pipe treatment issues are eliminated.

### Improved Relations with State Environmental Agencies

Sixteen state departments of environmental protection believe that an EMS may improve regulatory compliance and are considering ISO 14001 as fulfillment of various permit and other environmental operating requirements. These states are California, Colorado, Maryland, Massachusetts, Michigan, Minnesota, Nebraska, New Jersey, New York, North Carolina, Pennsylvania, South Carolina, Tennessee, Texas, Washington, and Wisconsin. Separately, a Multi-State Working Group (MSWG) on Environmental Management—composed of regulators from Arizona, California, Illinois, Massachusetts, Minnesota, North Carolina, Oregon, Pennsylvania, Texas, and Wisconsin—is exploring the potential of ISO 14001 to enhance public policies concerning environmental protection and pollution prevention.

## BENEFITS OF INTEGRATION

In mid-1998, nearly 26,000 North American companies were registered to ISO 9000 or QS-9000. Many of these companies plan to implement ISO 14001. Integrating ISO 14001 into an existing quality management system such as ISO 9001/2 has significant advantages.

Both ISO 14001 and ISO 9001/2 require a number of procedures that are virtually identical. The use of existing quality management procedures to fulfill ISO 14001 requirements eliminates redundancy and ensures consistency. Parallel systems, in which separate procedures are developed, often create confusion because nearly identical requirements must be addressed differently depending on whether a function (such as record keeping) is performed for the quality management or environmental management system.

The use of existing quality management procedures also creates significant savings in the cost of developing and implementing an EMS.

Still another advantage is the introduction of environmental management as a way of doing business. When the systems are integrated, there is less likelihood that the EMS will be viewed as a "program" that is primarily the responsibility of the environmental department. From an operational viewpoint, a fully integrated system creates an umbrella that covers all aspects of business, from product quality and customer service to maintaining operations in a safe and environmentally acceptable way.

The authors of ISO 14001 allude to the benefits of integration in that document's introduction, which states:

> [ISO 14001] shares common management system principles with the ISO 9000 series of quality system standards. Organizations may elect to use an existing management system consistent with the ISO 9000 series as a basis for its environmental management system. . . . The environmental management system requirements specified in [ISO 14001] do not need to be established independently of existing management system elements. In some cases, it will be possible to comply with the requirements by adapting existing management system elements.
>
> —ISO 14001, p. viii

Some companies worry that a downside to full integration is the potential for an organization to jeopardize its ISO 9001/2 certification during an audit because of inadequate performance on the environmental side, or vice versa. As this book goes to press, registrars have not determined how they will handle such situations.

Another concern about full integration pertains to the different primary customers of the two management systems. The primary customers of a QMS are the purchasers of the products and services offered by the company implementing the QMS. The primary customers of an EMS are those affected by the environmental impacts created by the operations and activities of the company implementing the EMS. A fully integrated system will address the concerns of both groups.

Chapter 2 compares the management principles common to ISO 14001 and ISO 9001/2.

# CHAPTER 2

## Quality Management
## and Environmental Management
## System Standard Similarities

Integration typically involves introducing ISO 14001 elements into a mature ISO 9001/2 quality management system (QMS). This requires an understanding of the similarities and differences between the two standards so that existing quality procedures and other activities can be used to fulfill environmental management system (EMS) requirements wherever possible. Figure 2.1 identifies elements with similar requirements.

Those ISO 9001/2 elements that are similar to ISO 14001 elements are presented in the sections that follow. Comparison of the two standards is organized according to ISO 9001/2 nomenclature. Discussion focuses on interpretation of ISO 14001 requirements. Unless otherwise noted, all references to an integrated system pertain to a fully integrated system.

Where the standards differ slightly, an integrated system must conform to the more stringent requirement. For example, ISO 9001/2 requires that a company establish a documented procedure for control of records while the records procedure required by ISO 14001 does not have to be documented. In a fully integrated system designed to fulfill requirements imposed by both standards, the procedure for records must be documented or it will not fulfill the ISO 9001/2 requirement.

| Requirement | ISO 9001/2 | ISO 14001 |
|---|---|---|
| Management responsibility | | |
| • policy | 4.1.1 | 4.2 |
| • responsibility and authority | 4.1.2.1 | 4.4.1 |
| • resources | 4.1.2.2 | 4.4.1 |
| • management representative | 4.1.2.3 | 4.4.1 |
| • management review | 4.1.3 | 4.6 |
| System documentation | 4.2.1 | 4.4.4 |
| Document and data control | 4.5 | 4.4.5 |
| Purchasing | 4.6 | 4.4.6c |
| Process control | 4.9 | 4.4.6a, b 4.5.1 |
| Control of inspection, measuring and test equipment | 4.11 | 4.5.1 |
| Corrective and preventive action | 4.14 | 4.5.2 |
| Control of records | 4.16 | 4.5.3 |
| Internal system audits | 4.17 | 4.5.4 |
| Training | 4.18 | 4.4.2 |

**Figure 2.1**   ISO 9001/2 and ISO 14001 Common Elements

## COMPARISON OF ISO 9001/2 AND ISO 14001

Both standards require a formal policy statement. The quality policy must be defined by "executive" management, while the environmental policy is the responsibility of "top" management. Both terms are intended to mean senior management with decision-making responsibility for the organization (i.e., company, division, business unit, or other functional unit) in which the quality management/environmental management system has been implemented. Although the policy statements can be written by committee, senior management must approve and issue the policy.

ISO 14001 is far more prescriptive than ISO 9001/2 concerning the content of the policy statement. Just as a quality policy must reflect organizational goals and customer needs and expectations, an environmental policy must be appropriate to a company's activities. Thus, the policy must be consonant with a company's environmental impacts.

| ISO 9001/2-1994 | ISO 14001-1996 |
|---|---|
| *4.1 Management responsibility*<br><br>*4.1.1 Quality policy*<br><br>The supplier's management with executive responsibility shall define and document its policy for quality, including objectives for quality and its commitment to quality. The quality policy shall be relevant to the supplier's organizational goals and the expectations and needs of its customers. The supplier shall ensure that this policy is understood, implemented, and maintained at all levels of the organization. | *4.2 Environmental policy*<br><br>Top management shall define the organization's environmental policy and ensure that it:<br><br>a) is appropriate to the nature, scale and environmental impacts of its activities, products, and services;<br><br>b) includes a commitment to continual improvement and prevention of pollution;<br><br>c) includes a commitment to comply with relevant environmental legislation and regulations and with other requirements to which the organization subscribes;<br><br>d) provides the framework for setting and reviewing environmental objectives and targets;<br><br>e) is documented, implemented, maintained and communicated to all employees;<br><br>f) is available to the public. |

Beyond the requirement for appropriateness, however, ISO 14001 mandates that four specific commitments be embodied in the environmental policy.

- Commitment to continual improvement—This requirement tends to be interpreted by many companies as a demand for continual improvement of environmental performance. ISO

14001 defines continual improvement as a process of enhancing the EMS to achieve improvements in overall environmental performance. Thus, the appropriate focus is improving the system which, in turn, will result in improved performance. Continual improvement of the EMS is evidenced through internal system audits, corrective and preventive actions that address identified system nonconformances, and management review of the EMS.

- Commitment to prevention of pollution—The phrase "prevention of pollution" was selected deliberately to differentiate it from "pollution prevention" as defined by the U.S. Pollution Prevention Act of 1990. ISO 14001 defines prevention of pollution as the use of processes, practices, materials, or products that avoid, reduce, or control pollution and may include recycling, treatment, process changes, control mechanisms, efficient use of resources, and material substitution. It does not place these practices in a hierarchy.

- Commitment to comply with relevant environmental legislation and regulations—ISO 14001 is not intended to increase or change a company's legal obligations. Conformance with the standard should occur in addition to compliance with applicable laws and regulations.

- Commitment to comply with other requirements—This alludes to any standard or industry code of practice that has been adopted voluntarily. Examples include
  - ISO 9000
  - ICC Business Charter for Sustainable Development
  - CMA Responsible Care® Program

Both the quality and environmental policies must be conveyed to employees throughout the organization. ISO 9001/2 requires that the policy is "understood," while ISO 14001 states that the policy must be "communicated." This can be accomplished in a variety of ways, including

- Presentation at meetings
- Distribution of wallet-size cards containing the policy
- Inclusion in training programs

- Display of posters or banners
- Publication in employee newsletter

This requirement that every employee must be made aware of the environmental policy is virtually identical to ISO 9001/2 because communication implies understanding. Thus, the common practice of displaying the policy in a public area of company buildings is likely to be inadequate for conveying its intent and importance. A typical audit question requires employees to explain the meaning of the environmental policy. If the only method used to communicate the policy is to post it on a wall, employees will not be able to explain its meaning.

An additional requirement imposed by ISO 14001 involves individuals outside of the organization. The environmental policy must be "made available" to the public. Although ISO 14001 does not define "the public," it does define "interested party" as any individual or group concerned with or affected by the environmental performance of an organization. This suggests that the policy must be disclosed to any individual or group that expresses an interest in it.

There is nothing to prevent a company from creating a "management policy" by revising its quality policy to incorporate environmental values. However, an integrated policy statement often proves cumbersome to write and difficult to communicate. If employees are familiar with an existing quality policy, significant revisions may be perceived to demonstrate a lack of management commitment to the original policy. This is one element where two separate statements are warranted.

Both standards require a clear articulation of responsibility and authority for all employees who are involved in any facet of quality or environmental management. In the context of ISO 9001/2 and ISO 14001, responsibility pertains to specific tasks while authority pertains to influence and power. Employees with responsibility do not necessarily have authority; therefore, the standards deliberately differentiate between these concepts.

Quality management systems typically provide this information in the quality manual. Additional detail often is found in supporting documentation such as organization charts, job descriptions, skills inventories, and employee performance objectives.

| ISO 9001/2-1994 | ISO 14001-1996 |
|---|---|
| *4.1.2.1 Responsibility and authority* | *4.4.1 Structure and responsibility* |
| The responsibility, authority, and the interrelation of personnel who manage, perform, and verify work affecting quality shall be defined and documented, particularly for personnel who need the organizational freedom and authority to: | (paragraph 1) Roles, responsibilities and authorities shall be defined, documented and communicated in order to facilitate effective environmental management. |
| a) initiate action to prevent the occurrence of any nonconformities relating to product, process, and quality system; | |
| b) identify and record any problems relating to the product, process, and quality system; | |
| c) initiate, recommend, or provide solutions through designated channels; | |
| d) verify the implementation of solutions; | |
| e) control further processing, delivery, or installation of nonconforming product until the deficiency or unsatisfactory condition has been corrected. | |

The quality manual and supporting documentation can be expanded to capture any additional functions with environmental responsibility and define the environmental responsibilities and authorities of all affected employees.

| ISO 9000-1994 | ISO 14001-1996 |
|---|---|
| *4.1.2.2 Resources* | *4.4.1 Structure and responsibility* |
| The supplier shall identify resource requirements and provide adequate resources, including the assignment of trained personnel (see 4.18), for management, performance of work and verification activities, including internal quality audits. | (paragraph 2) Management shall provide resources essential to the implementation and control of the environmental management system. Resources include human resources and specialized skills, technology and financial resources. |

To ensure that all system activities are fully implemented and maintained, both standards require that appropriate resources are provided. Resources fall into four categories—people, time, funding, and equipment.

It is difficult to verify whether sufficient resources are available and appropriately allocated to implement an integrated system. In one situation, 10 people with a 20 percent time commitment and a budget of $50,000 might be needed; in another, twice as many people might be insufficient.

Companies (and auditors!) should focus on *how* resource requirements are determined and evaluated rather than on absolute numbers. If the system is properly implemented and maintained, it is difficult to argue that resources are inadequate. If the system is not properly implemented and maintained, it is still difficult to ascribe deficiencies to inadequate resources.

Although ISO 14001 allows shared responsibility, ISO 9001/2 implies that a single individual must serve as the designated management representative. If the integrated system is to conform to both sets of requirements, a single management representative must be appointed. Typically, the QMS representative assumes the additional responsibility of environmental management.

| ISO 9000-1994 | ISO 14001-1996 |
|---|---|
| *4.1.2.3 Management representative* | *4.4.1 Structure and responsibility* |
| The supplier's management with executive responsibility shall appoint a member of the supplier's own management who, irrespective of other responsibilities, shall have defined authority for | (paragraph 3) The organization's top management shall appoint a specific management representative(s) who, irrespective of other responsibilities, shall have defined roles, responsibilities and authority for: |
| a) ensuring that a quality system is established, implemented and maintained in accordance with this standard, and | a) ensuring that environmental management system requirements are established, implemented and maintained in accordance with this standard; |
| b) reporting on the performance of the quality system to the supplier's management for review and as a basis for improvement of the quality system. | b) reporting on the performance of the environmental management system to top management for review and as a basis for improvement of the environmental management system. |
| NOTE 5 The responsibility of a management representative may also include liaison with external parties on matters relating to the supplier's quality system. | |

The experience of most companies, however, suggests that the QMS representative usually does not possess the requisite skills to adequately oversee the establishment, implementation, and maintenance of EMS requirements. To compensate, an individual experienced in environmental matters can work with this management representative to ensure that the integrated system does not omit any ISO 14001 requirements.

The purpose of the management review is to ensure that the quality and environmental management systems continue to be

| ISO 9000-1994 | ISO 14001-1996 |
|---|---|
| *4.1.3 Management review* | *4.6 Management review* |
| The supplier's management with executive responsibility shall review the quality system at defined intervals sufficient to ensure its continuing suitability and effectiveness in satisfying the requirements of this standard and the supplier's stated quality policy and objectives (see 4.1.1). Records of such reviews shall be maintained (see 4.16). | The organization's top management shall, at intervals it determines, review the environmental management system to ensure its continuing suitability, adequacy, and effectiveness. The management review process shall ensure that the necessary information is collected to allow management to carry out this evaluation. This review shall be documented.<br><br>The management review shall address the possible need for changes to policy, objectives and elements of the environmental management system in the light of environmental management system audit results, changing circumstances and the commitment to continual improvement. |

appropriate and capable of producing desired results. ISO 14001 specifies that the review must consider whether changes to the policy, objectives, and other elements of the EMS are needed.

In a partially integrated system, separate management reviews are conducted for the quality and environmental management systems. The review procedure may be virtually identical, although participants in the process and data used in conjunction with the review are likely to differ.

In a fully integrated system, a single management review that encompasses all system requirements is conducted. In this circumstance, the number of participants may increase while the data that support the review will expand significantly. This raises questions concerning the length and timing of review meetings.

Neither standard requires that all elements of the system be reviewed at once. Companies can employ a review process that occurs over some period of time—for example, quarterly reviews that focus on four or five selected elements—so long as the completed review (in this example, after four quarters) is comprehensive. Such an approach will allow for the possibility of different levels of maturity in the QMS and EMS. (See chapter 7 for additional information about management review.)

| ISO 9001/2-1994 | ISO 14001-1996 |
|---|---|
| *4.2.1 General*<br><br>The supplier shall establish, document, and maintain a quality system as a means of ensuring that product conforms to specified requirements. The supplier shall prepare a quality manual covering the requirements of this standard. The quality manual shall include or make reference to the quality-system procedures and outline the structure of the documentation used in the quality system. | *4.4.4 Environmental management system documentation*<br><br>The organization shall establish and maintain information, in paper or electronic form, to<br><br>a) describe the core elements of the management system and their interaction;<br><br>b) provide direction to related documentation. |

The terms "establish" and "maintain" appear throughout both standards. "Establish" means to institute or bring into existence, while "maintain" means to keep in an existing state or preserve from failure or decline.

ISO 9001/2 requires a quality manual that "covers" all requirements, while ISO 14001 is less prescriptive. The description of ISO 14001 core elements (that is, all numbered sub clauses in Clause 4 of the standard) does not have to be in the form of a manual. In a fully integrated system, the easiest approach is to modify the existing quality manual so that it describes the requirements contained in both standards.

In a partially integrated system, EMS documentation typically is an independent compilation that borrows from or references

| ISO 9000-1994 | ISO 14001-1996 |
|---|---|
| *4.2.2 Quality-system procedures*<br><br>The supplier shall<br><br>a)  prepare documented procedures consistent with the requirements of this standard and the supplier's stated quality policy; and<br><br>b)  effectively implement the quality system and its documented procedures.<br><br>For the purposes of this standard, the range and detail of the procedures that form part of the quality system depend on the complexity of the work, the methods used, and the skills and training needed by personnel involved in carrying out the activity.<br><br>NOTE 7 Documented procedures may make reference to work instructions that define how an activity is performed. | *4.1 General requirements*<br><br>The organization shall establish and maintain an environmental management system, the requirements of which are described in the whole of clause 4. |

ISO 9001/2 documentation. Documentation should be developed in a form that is useful to the company.

Related documentation (see chapters 4 and 5) also must be maintained in either paper or electronic form and may include

- Internal standards
- Operational procedures
- Organization charts
- Process information
- Site emergency plans

One of the distinct differences between the two standards is the requirement in ISO 9001/2 that all procedures be documented and the lack of required documentation in ISO 14001. The environmental management system standard specifies only three procedures that must be documented (see Figure 2.2)—operational control procedures (see 4.4.6a), the procedure to monitor and measure key characteristics of operations and activities that can have a significant environmental impact (see 4.5.1, paragraph 1) and the procedure to periodically evaluate compliance with relevant environmental legislation and regulations (see 4.5.1, paragraph 3).

| Procedures | Activities |
|---|---|
| Operating procedures for activities associated with significant environmental aspects [4.4.6]; Monitoring and measurement of activities that can have a significant environmental impact [4.5.1]; Periodic evaluation of regulatory compliance [4.5.1]. | Environmental policy [4.2]; Environmental objectives [4.3.3]; Roles, responsibilities, and authority [4.4.1]; Relevant communication from interested parties [4.4.3]; Decision regarding external communication about significant environmental aspects [4.4.3]; EMS documentation [4.4.4]; Calibration and maintenance of monitoring equipment [4.5.1]; Compliance audits [4.5.1]; Changes in any documented procedures [4.5.2]; Training [4.5.3]; Management review of the EMS [4.6]. |

Figure 2.2   ISO 14001 Requirements That Must Be Documented

Although ISO 14001 requires the establishment of 10 additional procedures, the standard does not require that these procedures be documented (see Figure 2.3). The authors strongly endorse

| Procedures | Activities |
| --- | --- |
| Identification of environmental aspects [4.3.1]; | Environmental management program [4.3.4]; |
| Identification of and access to legal and other requirements [4.3.2]; | Identification of training needs [4.4.2]. |
| Training reawareness, skills [4.4.2]; | |
| Internal communication [4.4.3]; | |
| Receiving, documenting, and responding to relevant communication from external interested parties [4.4.3]; | |
| Control of all documents [4.4.5]; | |
| Identifiable significant environmental aspects of goods and services used by the company [4.4.6]; | |
| Identification of potential for and response to accidents and emergencies [4.4.7]; | |
| Definition of responsibility and authority for addressing nonconformance and corrective/preventive action [4.5.2]; | |
| Identification, maintenance, and disposition of environmental records [4.5.3]; | |
| EMS audits [4.5.4]. | |

**Figure 2.3**    ISO 14001 Requirements That Do Not Have to Be Documented

documenting all procedures to ensure that they are understood and consistently followed. In an integrated system, all procedures will have to be documented. Otherwise, the system will not conform to ISO 9001/2 requirements.

ISO 14001 does not require an environmental management plan; however, it does require planning, which encompasses an understanding of all significant environmental impacts and developing objectives and targets to minimize those impacts.

An environmental aspect is defined as an element of an organization's activities, products, or services that can interact with the environment. An environmental impact is defined as any change to the environment, whether adverse or beneficial, wholly or partially resulting from an organization's activities, products, or services.

The purpose of this requirement is to ensure that the most significant environmental aspects and impacts of a company's activities are addressed as priorities. Companies must be able to provide objective evidence of

- Information about the environmental aspects and impacts associated with their operations and activities under normal, shut-down and start-up conditions, and accident/emergency situations; and
- Methods for obtaining and updating that information. Procedures could include checklists, interviews, direct inspection and measurement, or results of environmental compliance audits.

Information that has been developed for regulatory purposes can be used in fulfilling these requirements.

Objectives and targets must be documented and consistent with all commitments embodied in the environmental policy. Prevention of pollution is explicitly emphasized; therefore, objectives and targets should reflect this emphasis.

The ISO 14001 definition differs from the pollution prevention hierarchy contained in the Pollution Prevention Act (PPA) of 1990. The PPA emphasizes source reduction; ISO 14001 accepts avoidance, reduction, or *control* as equally acceptable approaches.

The standard does not require objectives and targets for every identified significant environmental aspect. Companies can develop objectives and targets for a subset of environmental aspects based on

| ISO 9001/2-1994 | ISO 14001-1996 |
|---|---|
| *4.2.3 Quality planning* | *4.3.1 Environmental aspects* |
| The supplier shall define and document how the requirements for quality will be met. Quality planning shall be consistent with all other requirements of a supplier's quality system and shall be documented in a format to suit the supplier's method of operation. The supplier shall give consideration to the following activities, as appropriate, in meeting the specified requirements for products, projects, or contracts:<br><br>a) the preparation of quality plans;<br><br>NOTE 8 The quality plans referred to (see 4.2.3a) may be in the form of a reference to the appropriate documented procedures that form an integral part of the supplier's quality system. | The organization shall establish and maintain (a) procedure(s) to identify the environmental aspects of its activities, products, or services that it can control and over which it can be expected to have an influence, in order to determine those which have or can have significant impacts on the environment. The organization shall ensure that the aspects related to these significant impacts are considered in setting its environmental objectives. The organization shall keep this information up-to-date.<br><br>*4.3.3 Objectives and targets*<br><br>The organization shall establish and maintain documented environmental objectives and targets, at each relevant function and level within the organization.<br>    When establishing and reviewing its objectives, an organization shall consider the legal and other requirements, its significant environmental aspects, its technological options, and its financial, operational and business requirements, and the views of interested parties.<br>    The objectives and targets shall be consistent with the environmental policy, including the commitment to prevention of pollution. |

consideration of legal and other requirements, significant environmental aspects, technological options, financial, operational, and business requirements, and the views of interested parties.

Establishing modest and attainable targets versus "stretch" targets that may result in better environmental performance than modest targets while falling short of the stipulated performance requirement has been a subject of debate. Both kinds of targets should be acceptable to an auditor, so long as the ISO 14001 requirements are met.

ISO 14001, Clause 4.5.1 Monitoring and measurement requires that all objectives and targets must be monitored. Companies will find it useful to select environmental performance indicators when they establish objectives and targets. Categories of environmental performance indicators, described in detail in ISO 14031 Environmental management—Environmental performance evaluation—Guidelines, are

- Management performance indicators—Provide information about managing matters such as training, legal requirements, resource allocation, purchasing, documentation, corrective action, and other similar issues that influence the organization's environmental performance.
- Operational performance indicators—Provide information about materials, natural resources, and other items used by the organization; design, installation, operation, and maintenance of physical facilities and equipment; products, by-products, and wastes; and other similar items related to the environmental performance of the organization's operations.
- Environmental condition indicators—Provide information about the local, regional, national, or global condition of the environment in which the organization conducts business. Although these indicators are not measures of a company's environmental performance, they can assist in establishing objectives and targets focused on prevention of pollution.

The information expressed by environmental performance indicators can be

- Absolute—Raw numbers without interpretation
- Relative—Information that has been interpreted on the basis of a separate piece of information, such as units of production

- Indexed—Information that has been interpreted on the basis of a percentage increase or decrease from a baseline year

All indicators should be understandable, relevant, valid (that is, they measure what they are intended to measure), and value-neutral. In some instances, information may be aggregated or weighted—care should be taken to ensure verifiability, consistency, and comparability.

In a fully integrated system, these environmental management planning activities are most easily accommodated in conjunction with the quality planning process that has been established to fulfill ISO 9001/2 requirements. In a partially integrated system, consideration should be given to keeping these activities separate from ISO 9001/2 planning efforts.

| ISO 9001/2-1994 | ISO 14001-1996 |
|---|---|
| *4.2.3 Quality planning*<br><br>The supplier shall define and document how the requirements for quality will be met. Quality planning shall be consistent with all other requirements of a supplier's quality system and shall be documented in a format to suit the supplier's method of operation. The supplier shall give consideration to the following activities, as appropriate, in meeting the specified requirements for products, projects, or contracts:<br><br>  b) the identification and acquisition of any controls, processes, equipment (including inspection and test equipment), fixtures, resources, and skills that may be needed to achieve the required policy; | *4.3.4 Environmental management programs*<br><br>The organization shall establish and maintain (a) program(s) for achieving its objectives and targets. It shall include<br><br>  a) designation of responsibility for achieving objectives and targets at each relevant function and level of the organization;<br><br>  b) the means and time-frame by which they are to be achieved.<br><br>If a project relates to new developments and new or modified activities, products or services, programs shall be amended where relevant to ensure that environmental management applies to such projects. |

Both standards require development of a plan for achieving all articulated goals, objectives, and targets. ISO 9001/2 requires that resources and skills be identified, while ISO 14001 explicitly mandates designated responsibilities, resources, and the time frame within which objectives and targets will be met.

Conformance with the ISO 9001/2 requirements is guided by ISO 8402, Quality management and quality assurance—Vocabulary, which states that quality planning covers

- Product planning—identifying, classifying and weighting the characteristics for quality as well as establishing the objectives, requirements for quality and constraints; and

- Managerial and operational planning—preparing the application of the quality system including organizing and scheduling

This information is captured in a quality plan, a document that depicts specific quality practices, resources, and sequence of activities relevant to a particular product, project, or contract.

The ISO 14001 requirement typically is fulfilled by a project management approach that delineates critical action steps, responsibilities, resources, timing, and milestones. Some companies will develop a single program that addresses all the action steps and responsibilities necessary to achieve multiple objectives and targets. Others will find greater value in developing a separate program for every objective. Either approach is acceptable.

In an integrated system, the quality plan provides a vehicle for assigning responsibility and delineating the practices, resources, sequence of activities, and timing relevant to every stated environmental objective and target.

The requirements concerning document control are virtually identical in both standards. Thus, the existing quality procedure can be used for controlling all internally generated and externally imposed documents required by the integrated system. Internal documents might include procedures, instructions, forms, and drawings; external documents might include customer-supplied specifications, voluntary standards, regulations, and Material Safety Data Sheets.

In ISO 14001, this element is intended to ensure that companies create and maintain documents in a way that supports effective

| ISO 9001/2-1994 | ISO 14001-1996 |
|---|---|
| *4.5.1 General* | *4.4.5 Document control* |
| The supplier shall establish and maintain documented procedures to control all documents and data that relate to the requirements of this standard including, to the extent applicable, documents of external origin such as standards and customer drawings. | The organization shall establish and maintain procedures for controlling all documents required by this standard to ensure that |
| *4.5.2 Document and data approval and issue* | a) they can be located; |
| The documents and data shall be reviewed and approved for adequacy by authorized personnel prior to issue. A master list or equivalent document-control procedure identifying the current revision status of documents shall be established and be readily available to preclude the use of invalid and/or obsolete documents.<br><br>    This control shall ensure that: | b) they are periodically reviewed, revised as necessary, and approved for adequacy by authorized personnel;<br><br>c) the current versions of relevant documents are available at all locations where operations essential to the effective functioning of the environmental management system are performed;<br><br>d) obsolete documents are promptly removed from all points of issue and points of use or otherwise assured against unintended use; |
| a) the pertinent issues of appropriate documents are available at all locations where operations essential to the effective functioning of the quality system are performed; | e) any obsolete documents retained for legal and/or knowledge preservation purposes are suitably identified. |

*(continued)*

| ISO 9001/2-1994 | ISO 14001-1996 |
|---|---|
| b)  invalid and/or obsolete documents are promptly removed from all points of issue or use, or otherwise assured against unintended use;<br><br>c)  any obsolete documents retained for legal and/or knowledge-preservation purposes are suitably identified.<br><br>*4.5.3 Document and data changes*<br><br>Changes to documents and data shall be reviewed and approved by the same functions/ organizations that performed the original review and approval, unless specifically designated otherwise. The designated functions/organizations shall have access to pertinent background information upon which to base their review and approval.<br><br>  Where practicable, the nature of the change shall be identified in the document of the appropriate attachments. | Documentation shall be legible, dated (with dates of revision), and readily identifiable, maintained in an orderly manner and retained for a specified period. Procedures and responsibilities shall be established and maintained concerning the creation and modification of the various types of document. |

implementation of the EMS and, by extension, improved environmental performance. Therefore, emphasis should be placed on supporting the EMS rather than on developing a complex document management system. ISO 9001/2 goes beyond ISO 14001 by incorporating data control into this element.

| ISO 9001/2-1994 | ISO 14001-1996 |
|---|---|
| *4.6 Purchasing* | *4.4.6 Operational control* |
| *4.6.1 General* | The organization shall identify those operations and activities that are associated with the identified significant environmental aspects in line with its policy, objectives and targets. The organization shall plan these activities, including maintenance, in order to ensure that they are carried out under specified conditions by: |
| The supplier shall establish and maintain documented procedures to ensure the purchased product (see 3.1) conforms to specified requirements. | |
| *4.6.2 Evaluation of subcontractors* | |
| The supplier shall: | |
|   a) evaluate and select subcontractors on the basis of their ability to meet subcontract requirements including the quality system and any specific quality-assurance requirements; |   c) establishing and maintaining procedures related to the identifiable significant environmental aspects of goods and services used by the organization and communicating relevant procedures and requirements to suppliers and contractors. |
|   b) define the type and extent of control exercised by the supplier over subcontractors. This shall be dependent upon the type of product, the impact of subcontracted product on the quality of final product, and, where applicable, on the quality audit reports and/or quality records of the previously demonstrated capability and performance of subcontractors; | |
|   c) establish and maintain quality records of acceptable subcontractors (see 4.16). | |

Under ISO 9001/2, evaluation of subcontractors addresses two separate concepts. First, purchased goods and services must meet stipulated quality requirements imposed by the purchasing company. Second, factors beyond quality, such as customer support services, financial stability, and delivery performance, are valid considerations.

ISO 14001 imposes similar requirements. Companies must consider the environmental aspects (and related impacts) of goods and services and determine whether procedures to control or minimize those impacts are warranted. Most companies have such procedures for the transport, storage, and disposal of hazardous waste. However, similar procedures often are lacking for more benign activities, such as construction, painting, janitorial services, and yard maintenance. ISO 14001 requires that companies understand the environmental aspects of such activities and ensure that appropriate procedures are communicated to subcontractors and suppliers.

One of the easiest ways to ensure that suppliers and contractors understand company requirements related to environmental aspects and follow established procedures is creation of an approved supplier/contractor list. This approach, which is ubiquitous in quality management systems, prevents an organization from contracting with companies that do not perform in an acceptable manner.

Three ISO 14001 elements address the process control concepts presented in ISO 9001/2. ISO 9001/2 specifies that documented procedures are necessary where their absence could adversely affect quality. Similarly, ISO 14001 requires documented procedures where their absence could lead to a deviation from the environmental policy, objectives, and targets. In both cases, the need for documented procedures is left to the discretion of the organization implementing the system.

In an integrated system, a company will strive to incorporate both quality and environmental concerns into a single procedure that addresses the activity of interest. This does not mean that all procedures and work instructions must be revised. In a quality management system, such procedures are necessary only for those activities that affect quality. In an environmental management system, documented procedures are necessary only for those operations and activities with significant environmental aspects. This means that only those activities that affect quality and have significant environmental impacts will be governed by an integrated procedure. Procedures for activities that affect quality but do not have significant

| ISO 9001/2-1994 | ISO 14001-1996 |
|---|---|
| *4.9 Process control* | *4.4.6 Operational control* |
| The supplier shall identify and plan the production, installation and servicing processes which directly affect quality and shall ensure that these processes are carried out under controlled conditions. Controlled conditions shall include the following: | The organization shall identify those operations and activities that are associated with the identified significant environmental aspects in line with its policy, objectives and targets. The organization shall plan these activities, including maintenance, in order to ensure that they are carried out under specified conditions by: |
| a) documented procedures defining the manner of production, installation, and servicing, where the absence of such procedures could adversely affect quality; | a) establishing and maintaining documented procedures to cover situations where their absence could lead to deviations from the environmental policy and the objectives and targets; |
| c) compliance with reference standards/codes, quality plans, and/or documented procedures; | b) stipulating operating criteria in the procedures; |
| d) monitoring and control of suitable process parameters and product characteristics; | *4.3.2 Legal and other requirements* |
| | The organization shall establish and maintain a procedure to identify and have access to legal and other requirements to which the organization subscribes, that are applicable to the environmental aspects of its activities, products or services. |

*(continued)*

| ISO 9001/2-1994 | ISO 14001-1996 |
|---|---|
| | **4.5.1 Monitoring and measurement** |
| | (paragraphs 1 and 3) The organization shall establish and maintain documented procedures to monitor and measure on a regular basis the key characteristics of its operations and activities that can have a significant impact on the environment. This shall include the recording of information to track performance, relevant operational controls, and conformance with the organization's objectives and targets. |
| | The organization shall establish and maintain a documented procedure for periodically evaluating compliance with relevant environmental legislation and regulations. |

environmental aspects will remain unchanged, while additional procedures will be developed for activities with significant environmental aspects but no effect on quality.

ISO 9001/2 stipulates compliance with reference standards and codes. ISO 14001 also addresses this concept of "other" voluntary requirements that the organization imposes upon itself. This is intended to elevate the importance of corporate commitments to voluntary standards or industry codes of practice. Companies that endorse voluntary "environmental improvement" initiatives must ensure that they are understood and implemented.

ISO 14001 also attempts to ensure that employees perform job-related activities in compliance with environmental legal requirements. A procedure must address how the company identifies and accesses existing legal requirements, and how it identifies new requirements or changes to existing requirements.

Identification of legal and other requirements is relatively straightforward. However, establishing "access to" identified requirements can be confusing. In the context of ISO 14001, accessible means capable of being used or seen (i.e., available). Thus, information about legal requirements could be located in the office of legal counsel or the EHS department; as long as such information can be obtained by individuals throughout the organization, it is considered accessible.

On a daily basis, employees typically do not need access to all identified legal and other requirements. They do have to know about any requirements that are related to their job responsibilities.

Finally, ISO 9001/2 requires monitoring and control of processes related to quality. ISO 14001 imposes a similar requirement for all activities with actual or potential significant environmental impacts. Their "key characteristics"—that is, those components that constitute environmental performance—must be monitored and measured. This means that all significant aspects and impacts will be tracked, even if specific objectives and targets have not been established for those aspects. A monitoring and measurement procedure limited to tracking conformance with environmental objectives and targets does not fulfill the intent of this requirement.

In addition, ISO 14001 requires companies to evaluate environmental regulatory compliance. In the United States, regulatory compliance is likely to be evaluated by performing compliance audits or analysis of monitoring information that is required by permits (such as water discharge samples).

| ISO 9001/2-1994 | ISO 14001-1996 |
|---|---|
| *4.11 Control of inspection, measuring, and test equipment* | *4.5.1 Monitoring and measurement* |
| *4.11.2 Control procedure* | (paragraph 2) Monitoring equipment shall be calibrated and maintained and records of this process shall be retained according to the organization's procedures. |
| The supplier shall: . . . | |
| b) identify all inspection, measuring, and test equipment that can affect product quality, and calibrate and adjust them at prescribed intervals, or prior to use, against certified equipment having a known valid relationship to internationally or nationally recognized standards. Where no such standards exist, the basis used for calibration shall be documented; | |
| e) maintain calibration records for inspection, measuring, and test equipment (see 4.16); | |

In an integrated system, the existing measurement equipment calibration procedure can be used to fulfill ISO 14001 requirements. This can be accomplished by broadening the scope of the procedure to include environmental monitoring equipment.

| ISO 9001/2-1994 | ISO 14001-1996 |
|---|---|
| *4.14 Corrective and preventive action* | *4.5.2 Nonconformance and corrective and preventive action* |
| *4.14.1 General* <br><br> The supplier shall establish and maintain documented procedures for implementing corrective and preventive action. <br><br>     Any corrective or preventive action taken to eliminate the causes or actual or potential nonconformities shall be to a degree appropriate to the magnitude of problems and commensurate with the risks encountered. <br><br>     The supplier shall implement and record any changes to the documented procedures resulting from corrective and preventive action. | The organization shall establish and maintain procedures for defining responsibility and authority for handling and investigating nonconformance, taking action to mitigate any impacts caused, and for initiating and completing corrective and preventive action. <br><br>     Any corrective or preventive action taken to eliminate the causes of actual and potential nonconformances shall be appropriate to the magnitude of problems and commensurate with the environmental impact encountered. <br><br>     The organization shall implement and record any changes in the documented procedures resulting from corrective and preventive action. |

    Both ISO 9001/2 and ISO 14001 require internal audits to ensure the effective functioning of the planned system (see section numbers 4.17 and 4.5.4, respectively). If internal audits reveal any nonconformances—that is, a failure to fulfill a stated requirement—the root cause of the nonconformance must be determined and actions taken to correct the identified problem and prevent it from recurring.

    The ISO 9001/2 procedure should be applicable to investigating deficiencies in the EMS.

| ISO 9001/2-1994 | ISO 14001-1996 |
|---|---|
| *4.16 Control of quality records* | *4.5.3 Records* |
| The suppliers shall establish and maintain documented procedures for identification, collection, indexing, access, filing, storage, maintenance, and disposition of quality records. | The organization shall establish and maintain procedures for the identification, maintenance and disposition of environmental records. These records shall include training records and the results of audits and reviews. |
| Quality records shall be maintained to demonstrate conformance to specified requirements and the effective operation of the quality system. Pertinent quality records from the subcontractor shall be an element of these data. | Environmental records shall be legible, identifiable and traceable to the activity, product or service involved. Environmental records shall be stored and maintained in such a way that they are readily retrievable and protected against damage, deterioration or loss. Their retention times shall be established and recorded. |
| All quality records shall be legible and shall be stored and retained in such a way that they are readily retrievable in facilities that provide a suitable environment to prevent damage or deterioration and to prevent loss. Retention times of quality records shall be established and recorded. Where agreed contractually, quality records shall be made available for evaluation by the customer or the customer's representative for an agreed period. | Records shall be maintained, as appropriate to the system and to the organization, to demonstrate conformance to the requirements of this standard. |
| NOTE 19 Records may be in the form of any type of media, such as hard copy or electronic media. | |

The ISO 9001/2 records procedure should be applicable to EMS records with only minor modifications. The records covered by the procedure must be expanded to include all records required by ISO 14001.

- Training records
- EMS audit results
- Management review of the EMS
- Decision regarding voluntary external communication
- Environmental performance data
- Operational controls data
- Progress in achieving objectives and targets
- Equipment calibration
- Equipment maintenance
- Corrective and preventive actions

Retention times must be stipulated for all records. Retention times imposed by environmental regulations must be considered—an organization can retain its records beyond the time required by regulations, but cannot dispose of records earlier than mandated.

It also is important to define "readily retrievable." The criticality of information contained in a record will contribute to the definition. Some records may be deemed readily retrievable if they can be accessed within several hours while others may require access within minutes.

Internal audits must be conducted on a regular basis to ensure that the system operates as intended. A fully integrated system will be examined through a single audit that looks at all requirements imposed by both ISO 9001/2 and ISO 14001 or a combination of smaller audits designed to evaluate the total system over a period of time.

Partially integrated systems typically are evaluated through two separate audits. One audit examines those procedures identified as quality procedures and relevant supporting records. The other examines the procedures that are linked to the EMS. If the EMS uses quality procedures to support required activities, such procedures will be audited twice—once in conjunction with the quality management system and once in conjunction with the EMS. Each of these audits may be accomplished by evaluating the system of interest with one audit that addresses all requirements or several smaller audits that evaluate a few requirements at a time. Additional information about internal system audits appears in chapter 6.

| ISO 9001/2-1994 | ISO 14001-1996 |
|---|---|
| *4.17 Internal quality audits*<br><br>The supplier shall establish and maintain documented procedures for planning and implementing internal quality audits to verify whether quality activities and related results comply with planned arrangements and to determine the effectiveness of the quality system.<br><br>Internal quality audits shall be scheduled on the basis of the status and importance of the activity to be audited and shall be carried out by personnel independent of those having direct responsibility for the activity being audited.<br><br>The results of the audits shall be recorded and brought to the attention of the personnel having responsibility in the area audited. The management personnel responsible for the area shall take timely corrective action on deficiencies found during the audit.<br><br>Follow-up audit activities shall verify and record the implementation and effectiveness of the corrective action taken (see 4.16). | *4.5.4 Environmental management system audit*<br><br>The organization shall establish and maintain (a) programme(s) and procedures for periodic environmental management system audits to be carried out, in order to<br><br>a)  determine whether or not the environmental management system<br><br>1)  conforms to planned arrangements for environmental management, including the requirements of this standard; and<br><br>2)  has been properly implemented and maintained; and<br><br>b)  provide information on the results of audits to management.<br><br>The organization's audit programme, including any schedule, shall be based on the environmental importance of the activity concerned and the results of previous audits. In order to be comprehensive, the audit procedures shall cover the audit scope, frequency and methodologies, as well as the responsibilities and requirements for conducting audits and reporting results. |

| ISO 9001/2-1994 | ISO 14001-1996 |
|---|---|
| *4.18 Training* | *4.4.2 Training, awareness and competence* |
| The supplier shall establish and maintain documented procedures for identifying training needs and provide for the training of all personnel performing activities affecting quality. Personnel performing specific assigned tasks shall be qualified on the basis of appropriate education, training and/or experience, as required. Appropriate records of training shall be maintained (see 4.16). | The organization shall identify training needs. It shall require that all personnel whose work may create a significant impact upon the environment have received appropriate training. |
| | It shall establish and maintain procedures to make its employees, or members, at each relevant function and level, aware of: |
| | a) the importance of conformance with the environmental policy and procedures and with the requirements of the environmental management system; |
| | b) the significant environmental impacts, actual or potential, of their work activities and the environmental benefits of improved personal performance; |

*(continued)*

| ISO 9001/2-1994 | ISO 14001-1996 |
|---|---|
| | c) their roles and responsibilities in achieving conformance with the environmental policy and procedures and with the requirements of the environmental management system, including emergency preparedness and response requirements; and |
| | d) the potential consequences of departure from specified operating procedures. |
| | Personnel performing the tasks which can cause significant environmental impacts shall be competent on the basis of appropriate education, training and/or experience. |

Both standards require identification of training needs and the provision of training to all employees whose work affects quality and/or can create a significant environmental impact. Training in and of itself is not mandatory; both standards acknowledge that proficiency can be obtained through education, training, and/or experience.

ISO 14001 imposes an awareness training requirement that is not present in ISO 9001/2. Employees at relevant functions and levels must be made aware of environmental impacts associated with their work activities and their roles in ensuring that procedures are followed.

If the existing quality training procedure is used in an integrated system, it will have to be modified to accommodate the awareness training requirement imposed by ISO 14001.

## ADDITIONAL ISO 14001 ELEMENTS

There are two ISO 14001 elements for which no similar ISO 9001/2 requirements exist. These are communication and emergency preparedness and response.

---

*4.4.3 Communication*

With regard to its environmental aspects and environmental management system, the organization shall establish and maintain procedures for

  a) internal communication between the various levels and functions of the organization;

  b) receiving, documenting and responding to relevant communication from external interested parties.

The organization shall consider processes for external communication on its significant environmental aspects and record its decision.

---

Two procedures are required. First, a company must establish a procedure for ensuring that information about the EMS is conveyed throughout the organization. It is important to differentiate between distribution and communication of information. The former sends out information without any effort to ascertain whether it has been received and understood by the intended audience. Printing the environmental policy in a company newsletter is an example of distribution—if employees do not read the newsletter, the policy will not have been communicated even though it was printed for all to see. The latter requires understanding of the information that is conveyed, regardless of the method by which it is transmitted.

Second, a company must have in place a procedure for dealing with communication that is initiated by external parties. Regardless of the communication medium—telephone, letter, E-mail, facsimile transmission, or personal contact—a procedure must be established to respond and to document what has occurred.

Separately, the organization must decide whether it wants to voluntarily share information with external parties about its significant environmental aspects. There is no requirement to communicate externally. However, a formal record of decision must indicate what the company has decided.

---

*4.4.7 Emergency preparedness and response*

The organization shall establish and maintain procedures to identify potential for and respond to accidents and emergency situations, and for preventing and mitigating the environmental impacts that may be associated with them. The organization shall review and revise, where necessary, its emergency preparedness and response procedures, in particular, after the occurrence of accidents or emergency situations.

The organization shall also periodically test such procedures where practicable.

---

This element requires an understanding of the materials and substances used in company operations that could create an environmental incident (e.g., chemical spill) and the natural phenomena (e.g., hurricane) and business activities (e.g., rail transport) that could result in such incidents. A formal plan for responding to identified potential incidents is required.

## ISO 9001/2 ELEMENTS WITH NO ISO 14001 OVERLAP

Ten ISO 9001/2 elements have no similarity to ISO 14001 requirements. These are

- 4.3 Contract review
- 4.4 Design control (ISO 9001 only)
- 4.7 Control of customer-supplied product
- 4.8 Product identification and traceability
- 4.10 Inspection and testing
- 4.12 Inspection and test status
- 4.13 Control of nonconforming product
- 4.15 Handling, storage, packaging, preservation, and delivery
- 4.19 Servicing
- 4.20 Statistical techniques

Because these elements have no relationship to EMS requirements, companies will take the same approach as if they were implementing a stand-alone quality system.

# CHAPTER 3

## Getting Started

Many organizations may feel that they are operating effectively and, therefore, the integration of the quality and environmental management systems does nothing more than create a great deal of unnecessary paperwork. These organizations often find that when they begin to integrate their systems, many procedures required by the EMS already exist as part of the QMS. The ability to use QMS procedures in support of EMS requirements actually reduces paperwork.

However, some organizations overrespond to the requirements and develop an integrated system that is more demanding and cumbersome than is necessary to conform with the requirements. This results in the mistaken impression that the integrated management system is a "paper-creating" system. The system that works best is the simplest system that will meet all the elements of the imposed standards.

Despite the often-repeated concern that company size affects the manner in which ISO 9001/2 and ISO 14001 are integrated, the authors' experience suggests that organizational structure is the critical differentiator. Companies in which totally separate groups handle quality and environmental issues are more likely to experience difficulty in achieving seamless integration than those in which a cross-functional team is responsible.

To ensure effective planning, management, implementation, and assessment of the integrated system, a clearly identified group within the organization must have responsibility and authority for the integrated system. Although the accomplishment of many of the tasks may not be the line responsibility of this group—certain tasks may be delegated to other individuals in or functions of the organization—it must be the responsibility of one group to monitor these tasks and ensure that all are accomplished effectively. Quality assurance personnel with assigned responsibility for the development and documentation of the QMS typically assume responsibility for the design and implementation of the integrated system.

Although the steps of integration are presented sequentially, some steps may overlap and parts of many steps may be going on at one time. Organizations are dynamic and business continues while the integrated system is being implemented. Before implementing such a system, it is advisable to prepare a master plan. This document is developed in the same manner as any other major business plan. Typical steps in such a plan are

- Identify EMS requirements
- Determine what exists in the QMS
- Develop procedures
- Implement the integrated system
- Verify implementation

### Identify EMS Requirements

It is important that each of the EMS requirements is clearly understood in relation to QMS requirements. It is for this reason that the first step is to evaluate what the company is currently doing and is capable of doing. This comparison, referred to as *gap analysis,* helps identify existing procedures and practices, evaluate these procedures and practices against the ISO 14001 requirements, and identify deficiencies or gaps. The easiest approach entails creating a matrix that depicts every ISO 14001 requirement and identifies similar QMS requirements (see Figure 3.1).

### Determine What Exists in the QMS

The next step is to obtain an inventory of existing quality procedures within the organization. For the purpose of this discussion, the term *procedures* includes policies, instructions, or other instruments that govern how personnel operate, conduct business, and perform activities.

Depending on the size of the organization, different methods may be used for collecting this inventory of procedures. Usually, the quality assurance organization is responsible for collecting written procedures. The quality organization may have to go to various

| ISO 14001 Requirements | ISO 9001/2 Requirements |
|---|---|
| Documented environmental policy [4.2] including commitments to continual improvement [4.2b], prevention of pollution [4.2b], and compliance with legal and other requirements [4.2c] | Documented quality policy [4.1.1] including objectives for quality and commitment to quality |
| Method to ensure that policy is implemented, maintained, and communicated to all employees [4.2e] | Method to ensure that policy is understood, implemented and maintained at all levels of the organization [4.1.1] |
| Method to ensure that policy is available to the public [4.2f] | |
| Procedure to identify the environmental aspects of activities, products, and services [4.3.1] | |
| Procedure to determine which environmental aspects have a significant impact on the environment [4.3.1] | |
| Method to keep aspects/impacts information up-to-date [4.3.1] | |
| Method to incorporate aspects/impacts into the setting of objectives and targets [4.3.1] | |
| Procedure to identify legal requirements [4.3.2] | |
| Method to ensure access to legal requirements [4.3.2] | |
| Procedure to identify other (voluntary) environmental requirements [4.3.2] | |
| Method to ensure access to other (voluntary) environmental requirements [4.3.2] | |

*The term method is used to identify an activity for which a procedure is not specified.

**Figure 3.1**   Matrix of ISO 14001 and Corresponding
ISO 9001/2 Requirements (continued)

| ISO 14001 Requirements | ISO 9001/2 Requirements |
|---|---|
| Method to establish environmental objectives and targets [4.3.3] | |
| Documented environmental objectives and targets [4.3.3] | Definition and documentation of how requirements for quality will be met [4.2.3] |
| Designation of responsibility for achieving objectives and targets [4.3.4] | Preparation of quality plans [4.2.3a] |
| Means of achieving environmental objectives and targets [4.3.4] | Preparation of quality plans [4.2.3a] |
| Time frame for achieving environmental objectives and targets [4.3.4] | Preparation of quality plans [4.2.3a] |
| Defined and documented roles, responsibility, and authorities of workers involved in the EMS [4.4.1] | Defined and documented responsibility, authority, and interrelation of personnel involved in the QMS [4.1.2.1] |
| Method to communicate roles, responsibility, and authorities of workers involved in the EMS [4.4.1] | |
| Provision of essential EMS resources [4.4.1] | Identification and provision of adequate QMS resources [4.1.2.2] |
| Appointment of and defined roles, responsibility, and authority for (a) specific management representative(s) [4.4.1] | Appointment of and defined authority for a management representative [4.1.2.3] |
| Method to identify training needs [4.4.2] | Procedure to identify training needs [4.18] |
| Method to provide identified training [4.4.2] | Procedure to provide identified training [4.18] |
| Procedure to provide awareness training [4.4.2a-d] | |

Figure 3.1   *continued*

| ISO 14001 Requirements | ISO 9001/2 Requirements |
|---|---|
| Method to evaluate competence of personnel performing tasks which can cause significant environmental impact [4.4.2] | Method to evaluate qualifications of personnel performing specific assigned tasks [4.18] |
| Procedure for internal communication [4.4.3a] | |
| Procedure for receiving, documenting, and responding to relevant communication from external interested parties [4.4.3b] | |
| Method to consider processes for external communication on significant environmental aspects [4.4.3] | |
| Record of decision regarding external communication on significant environmental aspects [4.4.3] | |
| Description of EMS elements [4.4.4a] | Quality manual [4.2.1] |
| Direction to EMS-related documentation [4.4.4b] | Inclusion or reference to quality system procedures [4.2.1] |
| Procedures to control EMS documents [4.4.5] | Procedures to control quality system documents and data [4.5] |
| Method to identify operations and activities with significant environmental aspects [4.4.6] | Method to identify processes which directly affect quality [4.9] |
| Documented procedures and work instructions [4.4.6a, b] | Documented procedures and work instructions [4.9a] |
| Procedures related to the significant environmental aspects of purchased goods and services [4.4.6c] | Procedures to ensure that purchased product conforms to specified requirements [4.6.1] |

Figure 3.1    *continued*

| ISO 14001 Requirements | ISO 9001/2 Requirements |
|---|---|
| Method to communicate procedures and requirements to suppliers and contractors [4.4.6c] | Evaluation and selection of subcontractors [4.6.2a] and defined control over subcontractors [4.6.2b] |
| Procedure to identify potential accidents and emergency situations [4.4.7] | |
| Procedures for responding to accidents and emergency situations [4.4.7] | |
| Procedure to monitor and measure operations and activities that can have significant environmental impact [4.5.1] | Method to monitor and control process parameters and product characteristics [4.9d] |
| Procedures to calibrate monitoring and measuring equipment [4.5.1] | Procedures to control, calibrate, and maintain inspection, measuring, and test equipment [4.11.1] |
| Procedure to evaluate regulatory compliance [4.5.1] | |
| Procedures for investigating system nonconformances and initiating and completing corrective and preventive action [4.5.2] | Procedures for corrective action [4.14.2] and preventive action [4.14.3] |
| Procedures to identify, maintain, and dispose of environmental records [4.5.2] | Procedures to identify, collect, index, access, file, store, maintain, and dispose of quality records [4.16] |
| Procedure for internal EMS audits [4.5.4] | Procedure for internal quality audits [4.17] |
| Method for management review [4.6] | Method for management review [4.1.3] |

Figure 3.1 *concluded*

work areas to find out how specific operations are controlled and why personnel take specific actions. In the case of written procedures, it is essential to confirm that they are being followed as written or, if not, how the activities to which the procedures apply are actually being done.

Unwritten procedures are often very strong in an organization and must be seriously considered in the planning effort and as an important part of the data being collected. In order to evaluate and document such established practices, it is necessary to interview personnel involved in their execution.

A detailed review of procedures and practices is now performed in order to identify those that address one or more of the EMS requirements listed in the matrix. This information is entered into an expanded version of the matrix to identify what existing procedures and practices can be used to fulfill the various EMS requirements (see Figure 3.2). The outcome of this activity identifies those EMS requirements for which procedures must be developed.

### Develop Procedures

The next step in the sequence is to develop procedures for the integrated system. This entails modifying existing QMS procedures and creating new procedures.

The degree of modification depends upon the specific QMS procedure. Typically, modification means changing the scope and responsibilities/authorities. A quality procedure for controlling records might be revised so that the array of records to which it applies now includes environmental records. Responsibility and authority for establishing retention times for environmental records might reside with the environment, health, and safety department while such responsibility and authority for quality records continues to reside with the quality assurance department. The creation of new procedures is discussed in chapter 5.

To ensure that all required procedures are addressed, responsibility must be assigned to the modification or creation of each identified procedure. This is most easily accomplished with a Procedure Assignment Log that lists every required procedure by number and title, the names of individuals who are responsible for every procedure, date of completion, and approval date and authorization (see Figure 3.3). Initially, only the procedure number and title, procedure

| ISO 14001 Requirements | ISO 9001/2 Requirements | Existing Procedure/Practice | | | Create New |
| --- | --- | --- | --- | --- | --- |
| | | No/Title | Use as Is | Modify | |
| Method to identify training needs [4.4.2] | Procedure to identify training needs [4.18] | QP-121 Training Skills Inventory | | ✓ | |
| Procedure to provide awareness training [4.4.2a–d] | | New employee orientation; Human Resources handbook | | | ✓ |

Figure 3.2   Expanded Gap Analysis Matrix

| | Procedure Number | Procedure Title | Procedure Coordinator | Date Written/Revised | Approval (name/date) | Date of Implementation |
| --- | --- | --- | --- | --- | --- | --- |
| 01 | SP-40.180 | Training | Jeff Lynn | Revised 6/15/98 | John Smith 6/20/98 | |
| 02 | SP-40.210 | Communication | Martin Good | New 6/24/98 | John Smith 6/28/98 | |
| 03 | | | | | | |

Figure 3.3   Procedure Assignment Log

coordinator name, and approval name will be entered. As procedures are finalized and approved, dates will be entered. The log also contains space to enter the date of implementation for each procedure. This information will be filled in later in the system implementation process.

Once procedures have been assigned, it is essential to create a timeline that establishes realistic deadlines for developing procedures and related work instructions. Time frames should be short enough to sustain interest and momentum, but long enough to avoid interfering with daily operational activities.

Establishing a timeline is little more than an exercise in simple math, as follows:

- Divide the procedures into two groups—those that will be revised and those that will be newly created. For this example, let's assume that 10 quality procedures will be revised and 8 procedures will be newly written.

- Estimate the number of person-hours required to revise an existing procedure (e.g., 3 people × 4 hours = 12 hours/ procedure).

- Estimate the number of person-hours required to create a new procedure (e.g., 4 people × 40 hours = 160 hours/procedure).

- Multiply estimated hours by the number of procedures.

    10 revised procedures at 12 hours = 120 hours
    8 new procedures at 160 hours = 1280 hours

- Many procedures are likely to require work instructions that provide detailed guidance on how to perform specific tasks (see chapter 4). Estimate the number of work instructions. For this example, 15 work instructions support the 10 quality procedures that will be revised and 36 work instructions are estimated to support the new procedures.

- Estimate the number of person-hours required to revise an existing work instruction (e.g., 3 people × 6 hours = 18 hours/ instruction).

- Estimate the number of person-hours required to create a new instruction (e.g., 5 people × 24 hours = 120 hours/ instruction).

- Multiply estimated hours by the number of instructions.

    15 revised instructions at 18 hours = 270 hours
    36 new instructions at 120 hours = 4320 hours

All of this information can be captured in a matrix (see Figure 3.4). To complete the timeline, additional information is required. An overview of integrated system requirements and planned arrangements must be prepared in the form of a manual (the integrated system manual is discussed in detail in chapter 4) and employees must be trained to use the revised and new procedures and instructions.

- Estimate the number of person-hours required to revise the quality manual and approve the new integrated system manual. For this example, 106 hours are required as follows: two people will devote a week to revisions (80 hours), two others will review the revision and provide feedback (6 hours), the original two will spend a day making some additional changes in response to that feedback (16 hours), and the manual will undergo a final review (4 hours).
- Estimate the person-hours required to train employees. For this example

    200 employees × 8 hours = 1600 hours
    50 employees × 12 hours = 600 hours

The information collected in the matrix (see Figure 3.4) provides sufficient information to determine how much time is required to develop, document, and implement the integrated system.

The example presented here requires nearly 6000 person-hours to develop procedures and instructions. Establishing realistic start and completion dates is dependent upon the number of employees who will be involved in the integration process and the amount of time they can devote to their integrated system responsibilities in a given week. The involvement of a large number of employees typically allows concurrent development of procedures and instructions, thereby shortening the calendar. A small number of employees tends to result in sequential development and, therefore, a longer calendar. For example, if the same three people must revise all 10 procedures, they can only do one at a time. If they do one procedure a week, they will need 10 weeks and will miss their assigned deadline. However, if five teams of three are involved, five procedures can be revised concurrently. If

| Activity | Estimated Effort | | | Start | Finish |
|---|---|---|---|---|---|
| | People | × Hours | × Number | = Total Hours | | |
| Revise procedures | 3 | 4 | 10 | 120 | 02/01/99 | 03/31/99 |
| Create new procedures | 4 | 40 | 8 | 1,280 | 02/01/99 | 04/30/99 |
| Revise instructions | 3 | 6 | 15 | 270 | 04/01/99 | 06/30/99 |
| Create new instructions | 5 | 24 | 36 | 4,320 | 05/01/99 | 08/31/99 |
| Revise manual | 2 | 48 | | 96 | 05/01/99 | 05/31/99 |
| | 2 | 5 | | 10 | | |
| Train employees | 200 | 8 | | 1,600 | 09/01/99 | 10/31/99 |
| | 50 | 12 | | 600 | 09/01/99 | 11/15/99 |
| Total | | | | 8,296 | | |

Figure 3.4   Activity Schedule

each team completes one procedure a week, all 10 will be done in two weeks, well ahead of the imposed deadline.

The estimated schedule in Figure 3.4 depicts 5990 hours of work in a 30-week (or 1200-hour) period. If employees can devote 25 percent of their time to establishing procedures and instructions, 20 employees must be involved. A 20 percent time commitment means that 25 employees will have to participate.

The time required to complete the steps described depends on the number of existing procedures that can be used as written or with minor modification and available resources. The authors' experience suggests that nine months is typical, although some companies have achieved integration in as few as six months.

### Implement and Verify the Integrated System

The next step in this sequence of activities is the implementation of both revised and new procedures and instructions. This includes personnel orientation and training, correcting errors in the system, verifying correctness and adequacy of instructions and procedures, and keeping these documents current.

After an agreed period, an internal audit must be performed to verify implementation and identify any procedural problems that may have arisen. Once full conformance with a procedure is verified, that procedure is entered into a master audit schedule for periodic review. The audit procedure is the mechanism by which procedures are kept current and conformance is assured.

As each element of the integrated management system is reviewed, a decision must be made whenever there is a discrepancy between what has been planned and what is actually taking place. A thorough review of the cause of any nonconformance should be made and, if necessary, the system should be adjusted to meet the requirements. After this adjustment, the implementation of the changes must be audited. This process of review, adjust, implement, and audit is continuous.

Once all procedures required by both the EMS and QMS standards have been implemented and verified, system integration has been achieved. Continued effective auditing will assure continued conformance.

The remaining chapters in this book explain, among other things, how to document and audit the integrated system. Companies that start with the gap analysis described in this chapter in order to leverage those facets of the QMS that overlap with ISO 14001 requirements and allocate resources to fulfilling EMS requirements with little or no overlap to the QMS will be well on the way to developing and implementing an effective integrated system.

# CHAPTER 4

## Documenting the Integrated Management System

Both ISO 9001/2 and ISO 14001 require formal documentation of the system. ISO 9001/2 requires a manual that covers all requirements contained in the standard (see clause 4.2.1), while ISO 14001 specifies a description of the core elements of the environmental management system (EMS) (see clause 4.4.4).

### DOCUMENTATION LEVELS

Four types of documents typically are employed in the documentation of a management system. The first level of this hierarchy is the System Manual, which provides a description of the system. The second level contains system-level procedures. Work instructions comprise the third level, while records and forms (fourth-level documents) support the entire system. The formats of these documents are as varied as the organizations that develop them.

#### The Management System Manual

The purpose of the manual is to communicate a company's policies, identify the quality and environmental elements that are included in the system, and define who has the responsibility and authority for controlling the system.

ISO 14001 does not require that the Level 1 document be in the form of a manual. The standard states that organizations must describe the core elements of the management system in paper or electronic form. However, ISO 90001 requires that the system description is in the form of a manual. Therefore, a fully integrated system will employ a manual.

As the backbone of the management system, the manual provides the foundation for developing procedures and instructions. It identifies what specific requirements are controlled by procedures and/or work instructions and references those procedures and instructions so that a reader can locate related documents.

There is no standard format for a system manual. However, the following elements should be included.

- Table of Contents—Quality manuals typically present system elements in the numerical order employed by ISO 9001/2, that is, 4.1 through 4.20. This numbering sequence often is retained when ISO 14001 elements are integrated into an existing quality management system manual. Because ISO 14001 uses a different numerical sequence, readers can find it difficult to locate information related to environmental elements of the system. To avoid confusion, the manual can provide a table of contents that cross-references, by number, the elements from both standards.

- Quality Policy—The quality policy conveys a company's commitment to quality and, therefore, provides guidance for how specific system elements will be implemented.

- Environmental Policy—The environmental policy commits an organization to prevention of pollution. It provides a framework for establishing environmental objectives and targets.

- Organizational Structure—The organizational entity to which the system applies should be described. Any functional units that are excluded from the scope of the system should be clearly delineated.

- Authorities and Responsibilities—Key personnel with defined roles for implementing and maintaining the system should be identified by title.

- System Elements—All elements required by the guiding standards should be described.

- References—All related documentation should be identified
  so that the reader can obtain additional detail if desired.
  System-level procedures, work instructions, or other
  documents such as process flow diagrams, that support
  implementation of system elements should be included.

The manual must reflect the implementing company's own system and, therefore, will be unique. Some companies are tempted to use a generic manual developed by a consultant or borrow another company's manual and modify the language. This is an incredibly bad approach. Such manuals do not reflect the actual practices of the *borrowing* company and so do not describe the system that has actually been implemented. The manual must faithfully reflect an organization's commitment and accurately describe how it intends to control system elements.

Companies that are ISO-9001/2 registered typically use the existing quality manual as the basis of an integrated system manual. Rather than create a new manual, they insert language at appropriate points to expand discussion such that all required EMS elements are addressed (see Figure 4.1). The advantage of this approach is a single manual that encompasses all requirements.

There are several disadvantages. This approach tends to retain the section numbers contained in the original manual which correspond to the clause numbers in ISO 9001/2. This can create confusion for users who are familiar with ISO 14001 numbering and may not know how to locate a corresponding section by ISO 9001/2 numbering. A table of contents or index that cross-references the sections is helpful.

Other disadvantages are the tendency to force-fit elements together and the possibility that modification may jeopardize quality registration if changes to the manual are neither understood nor accepted by a registrar.

Integrating ISO 14001 into a QS-9000 manual differs in two areas. QS-9000 requires a business plan with accompanying goals (clause 4.1.4). The ISO 14001 elements pertaining to objectives and targets (clause 4.3.3) and environmental management program (clause 4.3.4) are easily integrated into this section (see Figure 4.2).

QS-9000 also makes specific reference to environmental regulations (clause 4.9c in the second edition and clause 4.6.1, third edition).

| Existing ISO 9001/2 Sections | Integrated ISO 14001 Sections |
|---|---|
| 4.1.1 Quality policy | 4.2 Environmental policy |
| 4.1.2.1 Responsibility and authority | 4.4.1 Structure and responsibility, ¶1 |
| 4.1.2.2 Resources | 4.4.1 Structure and responsibility, ¶2 |
| 4.1.2.3 Management representative | 4.4.1 Structure and responsibility, ¶3 |
| 4.1.3 Management review | 4.6 Management review |
| 4.2.1 General quality system | 4.1 General EMS<br>4.4.4 EMS documentation |
| 4.2.3 Quality planning | 4.3.1 Environmental aspects<br>4.3.2 Legal requirements<br>4.3.3 Objectives and targets<br>4.3.4 Environmental mgt. program |
| 4.5 Document and data control | 4.4.5 Document control |
| 4.6 Purchasing | 4.4.6c Operational control |
| 4.9a Process control (procedures) | 4.4.6a, b Operational control |
| 4.9c Process control | 4.5.1 Monitoring and measurement, ¶3 |
| 4.9d Process control (monitoring) | 4.5.1 Monitoring and measurement, ¶1 |
| 4.11 Control of . . . equipment | 4.5.1 Monitoring and measurement, ¶2 |
| 4.14 Corrective and preventive action | 4.5.2 Nonconformance and corrective and preventive action |
| 4.16 Control of quality records | 4.5.3 Records |
| 4.17 Internal quality audits | 4.5.4 EMS audits |
| 4.18 Training | 4.4.2 Training, awareness, and competence |
|  | 4.4.3 Communication |
|  | 4.4.7 Emergency preparedness and response |

**Figure 4.1**    Suggested Integration for Common Elements of ISO 9001/2 and ISO 14001

| Existing QS-9000 Sections (Third ed.) | Integrated ISO 14001 Sections |
|---|---|
| 4.1.1 Quality policy | 4.2 Environmental policy |
| 4.1.2.1 Responsibility and authority | 4.4.1 Structure and responsibility, ¶1 |
| 4.1.2.2 Resources | 4.4.1 Structure and responsibility, ¶2 |
| 4.1.2.3 Management representative | 4.4.1 Structure and responsibility, ¶3 |
| 4.1.3 Management review | 4.6 Management review |
| 4.1.4 Business plan | 4.3.3 Objectives and targets 4.3.4 Environmental mgt. program |
| 4.2.1 General quality system | 4.1 General EMS 4.4.4 EMS documentation |
| 4.2.3 Quality planning | 4.3.1 Environmental aspects |
| 4.5 Document and data control | 4.4.5 Document control |
| 4.6.1 General purchasing (government, safety, and environmental regulations) | 4.3.2 Legal requirements 4.5.1 Monitoring and measurement, ¶3 |
| 4.6.2b Evaluation of subcontractors | 4.4.6c Operational control |
| 4.9a Process control (procedures) | 4.4.6a, b Operational control |
| 4.9d Process control (monitoring) | 4.5.1 Monitoring and measurement, ¶1 |
| 4.11 Control of . . . equipment | 4.5.1 Monitoring and measurement, ¶2 |
| 4.14 Corrective and preventive action | 4.5.2 Nonconformance and corrective and preventive action |
| 4.16 Control of quality records | 4.5.3 Records |
| 4.17 Internal quality audits | 4.5.4 EMS audits |
| 4.18 Training | 4.4.2 Training, awareness, and competence |
|  | 4.4.3 Communication |
|  | 4.4.7 Emergency preparedness and response |

**Figure 4.2** Suggested Integration for Common Elements of QS-9000 and ISO 14001

Identification of legal requirements (ISO 14001, clause 4.3.2) fits well into this section of the manual.

The ISO 14001 elements on communication (clause 4.4.3) and emergency preparedness and response (clause 4.4.7) do not fit easily into any ISO 9001/2 or QS-9000 elements. These sections are most easily handled by creating two additional sections in the manual to follow the existing, revised sections.

A different approach to integration entails organizing the elements in both standards around the concepts they embody without relying on the numbering system embodied in either (see Figure 4.3).

| Issues | ISO 9001/2 | ISO 14001 |
|---|---|---|
| I.  Scope | | |
| II.  Management System | | |
|    A.    Policy | 4.1.1 | 4.2 |
|    B.    Planning | 4.2.3 | 4.3.3; 4.3.4 |
|    C.    Responsibility, Authority, and Structure | 4.1.2 | 4.4.1 |
|    D.    Implementation | 4.2 | 4.4.4 |
|    E.    Audits | 4.17 | 4.5.4 |
|    F.    Corrective and Preventive Action | 4.14 | 4.5.2 |
|    G.    Management Review | 4.1.3 | 4.6 |
| III.  Management System Support Activities | | |
|    A.    Document Control | 4.5 | 4.4.5 |
|    B.    Training | 4.18 | 4.4.2 |
|    C.    External Requirements | 4.3 | 4.3.2 |
|    D.    Internal Controls | 4.9 | 4.4.6 |
|    E.    Records | 4.16 | 4.5.3 |
|    F.    Monitoring and Measurement | 4.20 | 4.5.1 |
|    G.    Communication | | 4.4.3 |

Figure 4.3   Integrated Manual Organized by Concepts *(continued)*

| Issues | ISO 9001/2 | ISO 14001 |
|---|---|---|
| IV.  Production Support Activities | | |
|  A.  Design Control | 4.4 | |
|  B.  Environmental Aspect | | 4.3.1 |
|  C.  Purchasing | 4.6 | 4.4.6, ¶3 |
|  D.  Customer-Supplied Product | 4.7 | |
|  E.  Product Identification and Traceability | 4.8 | |
|  F.  Inspection and Testing | 4.10 | |
|  G.  Inspection and Test Status | 4.12 | |
|  H.  Control of Nonconforming Product | 4.13 | |
|  I.  Handling, Storage, Packaging, Preservation, and Delivery | 4.15 | |
|  J.  Servicing | 4.19 | |
|  K.  Calibration of Equipment | 4.11 | 4.5.1, ¶2 |
|  L.  Emergency Preparedness and Response | | 4.4.7 |

**Figure 4.3**  *concluded*

### System-Level Procedures

The second tier of documentation consists of system-level procedures, which describe the manner in which the system (described in the manual) will be implemented. A common misconception is that procedures describe *how* things are to be done. In fact, that is the purpose of work instructions. Procedures describe *what* is to be done, as well as why, when, where, and by whom. Calibration of inspection, measuring, and test equipment is illustrative.

• What—Depicts steps that must be followed, e.g.:
  1. Identify equipment requiring calibration
  2. Send to test department
  3. Log and identify

4. Calibrate and record
5. Return
6. Issue for use

The procedure does not describe how each step is to be accomplished. Separate work instructions should be developed where such explanation is necessary (e.g., calibrate and record).

- Why—Explains the purpose of the procedure, e.g., assures that all inspection, measuring, and test equipment used by production for activities with significant environmental impact is controlled, calibrated, and adjusted to maintain necessary accuracy

- When—Defines the conditions under which the procedure is to be implemented. Information can be presented on the basis of time (e.g., every six weeks) or precipitating event (e.g., receipt of newly purchased equipment).

- Where—Identifies the locations affected by the procedure, e.g., test equipment used for activities regulated by operating permits and for fabrication and assembly activities with significant environmental impacts

- Who—Identifies the function responsible for each step in the procedure, e.g.:
  1. Identify equipment requiring calibration—Fabrication department
  2. Send to test department—Fabrication department
  3. Log and identify—Test department
  4. Calibrate and record—Test department
  5. Return—Test department
  6. Issue for use—Fabrication department

System-level procedures are interdepartmental and, therefore, general. Each step identifies an activity performed by a department or other functional unit within the organization. Chapter 5 provides additional information about developing procedures for an integrated system.

### Instructions

The third tier of system documentation, instructions, provides detailed explanation on how to perform specific tasks. In contrast to procedures which are general in nature and explain the interaction of functional departments, instructions are specific and describe how individual tasks are to be performed.

It is critical that instructions are understood by their intended users. Don't be misled by the concept of reading level. Instructions written to an eighth-grade reading level will not necessarily be understood by workers who read at that level even though they will be able to read all the words. Consider the following sentence: The digital ossicle coalesces with the basal extremity; concurrently the basal extremity amalgamates with the astragalus. You probably read each of the words but did not understand that we were attempting to explain that the toe bone's connected to the foot bone and the foot bone's connected to the ankle bone. Consider replacing words with diagrams, drawings, icons, or other pictorial representations.

Instructions typically include the following information.

- Header—Contains identifying information required by ISO 9001/2, clause 4.5 Document and data control and ISO 14001, clause 4.4.5 Document control
- Equipment Required—Lists all equipment necessary to complete the task
- Safety Precautions—Warns of hazards, details necessary safeguards, and lists required safety equipment
- Steps—Explains each step in sequence and in sufficient detail to assure that every worker using the instruction will perform the task the same way
- Flow chart—Provides a graphic depiction of the steps

### Records

The fourth and final level of documentation provides the objective evidence, or proof, that a procedure, instruction, or other activity has been performed. Records can take numerous forms, including tables, graphs, drawings, and reports. Procedures and work instructions should stipulate specific records that are to be generated in conjunction with the activity described.

All records that pertain to the system must be controlled by the requirements specified in the guiding standards. Procedures for identification, collection, indexing, access, filing, storage, maintenance, retention, and disposition must be established.

## A FINAL WORD

The documented management system should be designed to assist the organization in assuring consistency within processes. The best approach for documenting a system is to start by evaluating what actually is being done. However, just because certain procedures and practices are in use does not mean that they are efficient. All procedures should be improved, if necessary, by eliminating redundancies and non–value added activities. Once procedures have been enhanced, supporting instructions and forms should be developed. Only then should the organization develop its manual.

# CHAPTER 5

## Combined Procedures

The purpose of a procedure—defined by ISO 8402, Quality management and quality assurance–Vocabulary, as "a specified way to perform an activity"—is to ensure that the activity in question is performed consistently (see chapter 4 for additional information).

ISO 9001/2 requires that organizations must prepare documented procedures consistent with the requirements of the standard (clause 4.2.2a). Specific reference is made to more than 20 documented procedures throughout the remainder of the standard.

- Contract review (4.3.1)
- Control and verification of product design (4.4.1)
- Control of documents and data (4.5.1)
- Conformance of purchased product to specified requirements (4.6.1)
- Verification, storage, and maintenance of customer-supplied product (4.7)
- Product identification ( 4.8)
- Identification of individual product or batches (4.8)
- Control of production, installation, and servicing processes (4.9a)
- Incoming, in-process, and final inspection and testing (4.10)
- Calibration and maintenance of inspection, measuring, and test equipment (4.11.1)
- Control of nonconforming product (4.13.1)
- Corrective action (4.14.2)
- Preventive action (4.14.3)

- Handling, storage, packaging, preservation, and delivery of product (4.15)
- Identification, collection, indexing, access, filing, storage, maintenance, and disposition of records (4.16)
- Planning and implementation of internal quality audits (4.17)
- Identification of training needs (4.18)
- Provision of training (4.18)
- Performance of servicing activities (4.19)
- Implementation of statistical techniques (4.20)

ISO 14001 also requires organizations to establish and maintain procedures. However, the standard specifies that procedures must be documented in only three clauses.

- Operating and maintenance criteria for activities associated with significant environmental aspects (4.4.6a)
- Monitoring and measurement of activities that can have a significant impact on the environment (4.5.1)
- Evaluation of regulatory compliance (4.5.1)

All other mention in ISO 14001 refers to *procedures* rather than *documented procedures,* a deliberate distinction made in response to the often-voiced concern that ISO 9001/2 can, and often does, become little more than a paperwork exercise. Hoping to deflect similar criticism, the writers of ISO 14001 have left it to companies to decide how much documentation is necessary in order to focus resources on designing and implementing an effective system.

In fact, most companies implementing ISO 14001 do document their procedures despite the failure of ISO 14001 to mandate this activity. Such documentation ensures common understanding and consistent implementation throughout the organization. It also ensures that the system will operate effectively in the absence of key employees.

Companies that elect to fully integrate the quality and environmental management systems will have to document all procedures. Otherwise, the system will not conform to the ISO 9001/2 general requirement for documented procedures in section 4.2.2a nor the specific requirements throughout section 4. Companies pursuing partial integration will have to document all procedures common to both standards. However, those unique to ISO 14001 (e.g., identification of environmental aspects) do not have to be documented. The authors believe that all procedures should be documented to ensure common understanding and consistent implementation throughout the organization.

Where both standards require virtually the same procedure, it makes sense to create one procedure that can be used to fulfill both sets of requirements. The ISO 9001/2 and ISO 14001 elements with similar requirements and, therefore, for which single, combined procedures can be established are illustrated in Figure 5.1.

| Procedures | ISO 9001/2 | ISO 14001 |
|---|---|---|
| Document and data control | 4.5.1 | 4.4.5 |
| Evaluation of subcontractors | 4.6.2 | 4.4.6c |
| Process control/operating conditions | 4.9a | 4.4.6a, b |
| Monitoring | 4.9d | 4.5.1, ¶1 |
| Calibration of measuring equipment | 4.11 | 4.5.1, ¶2 |
| Corrective and preventive action | 4.14 | 4.5.2 |
| Records control | 4.16 | 4.5.3 |
| Internal system audits | 4.17 | 4.5.4 |
| Training | 4.18 | 4.4.2 |

**Figure 5.1**   Integrated Procedures

### *Writing Procedures*

The first task to be accomplished entails determining what procedures are needed. The best way to accomplish this is to create a flow chart of the major processes in the organization. This is most easily accomplished by walking through company operations in sequence from beginning to end. What initiates the operation (e.g., customer order), what happens after initiation (e.g., materials are ordered, materials are received, product is manufactured, inspected, and shipped), and what concludes the operation (e.g., invoice is sent, payment is received)?

Every process identified on the flow chart should then be examined to determine whether specific procedures are required. For example, is a procedure necessary for ordering materials or shipping finished product?

The completed flow chart should be compared to the requirements contained in ISO 9001/2 and ISO 14001. All procedures specified by the standards should be included on the flow chart. If specified procedures are missing, they should be added. Between 35 and 45 procedures are typically needed for an integrated system.

This exercise ensures that all operational activities that must be controlled are identified. The flow chart becomes a tool for developing system-level procedures.

The second step is to determine whether procedures already exist for any of the processes identified on the flow chart. For each existing procedure, observe employees who use the procedure and document exactly what is being done. Actual practice should provide the basis for determining whether changes are needed. Once a procedure has been modified, again observe and document what is being done. Continue to modify the procedure until it accomplishes what is intended. This approach provides an opportunity to eliminate or update steps in a procedure that are inadequate, unnecessary, or inefficient. Only then should it be formalized in writing as required by the document control procedure.

There is no one correct format for a procedure. Typical elements contained in a procedure are

- Header—Contains identifying information required by ISO 9001/2, clause 4.5 Document and data control and ISO 14001, clause 4.4.5 Document control (see Figure 5.2)

| Mega Manufacturing Quality System Procedure | | Procedure No.: 40.110 | |
|---|---|---|---|
| Subject: | Control of Inspection, Measuring, and Test Equipment | Page: | 1 of 4 |
| | | Revision: | Original |
| | | Effective Date: | Jun 15, 1998 |
| Prepared by: | John Doe Test Dept. Supervisor | Approved by: | Jane Smith VP Quality Assurance |
| Date: | May 12, 1998 | Date: | May 25, 1998 |

Figure 5.2    Example of a Procedure Header

- Purpose—Explains why the procedure is being implemented
- Scope—Functional units or individuals to which the procedure applies
- Definitions—Identifies unfamiliar words, abbreviations, acronyms, and symbols used in the procedure
- References—Identifies related information such as the section of the standard addressed by the procedure
- Procedure—Addresses each step and identifies the function that is responsible for its achievement
- Records, Forms, Reports—Identifies any documentation required by the procedure
- Flow chart—Pictorially depicts all steps in the procedure

### Modifying Existing Procedures

In an integrated system, existing quality system procedures provide the foundation upon which environmental management procedures are built. Although some new procedures will have to be developed for those ISO 14001 requirements that do not appear in the quality management system (e.g., identification of environmental aspects, communication), many requirements can be addressed by modifying a quality procedure.

The most effective approach for modifying an existing procedure involves the use of cross-functional teams composed of employees who will implement the procedure. The team should walk through each step in the procedure to determine whether the wording is limited to quality assurance issues or broad enough to accommodate requirements imposed by ISO 14001.

To illustrate, Mega Manufacturing's Quality System Procedure #40.180, Control of Training, is presented to see whether it fulfills all requirements contained in ISO 14001, clause 4.4.2, Training, Awareness, and Competence and, if not, how it could be revised. The procedures presented here and elsewhere in this book are actual procedures used by an ISO 9002-registered company. Their purpose is intended solely to illustrate how existing quality procedures can be revised to fulfill EMS requirements while maintaining compliance to QMS requirements.

The cross-functional team assembled to review this training procedure in all likelihood would include

- Training manager—Responsible for managing the Mega Manufacturing training program, maintaining training files, identifying trainers and course providers, and identifying training needs
- Production managers and supervisors—Responsible for identifying employee training needs, conducting on-the-job training, and creating training records
- Executive staff members—Responsible for identifying employee training needs
- Training subcontractor—Responsible for conducting training and/or certifying employees
- Executive secretary—Responsible for travel arrangements related to off-site employee training
- Purchasing—Responsible for developing purchase order for off-site training

Language from the quality training procedure is set off in boxes. Discussion of changes follows each box.

---

**1.0 Purpose**

The purpose of this procedure is to identify employee training needs and to provide the training required to ensure quality of product and service and to satisfy the identified needs.

---

ISO 14001 requires identification of training needs and the provision of training to satisfy identified needs. Thus, the stated purpose as it relates to these two activities accommodates ISO 14001 requirements and does not have to be changed. The statement limits training, however, to ensuring quality of product and service. This wording is too narrowly focused to address ISO 14001 requirements, which stipulate that training is necessary for employees whose work may create a significant environmental impact. Employees at each relevant function and level must be made aware of the environmental management system and their roles in assuring its successful implementation. The purpose could be revised as:

The purpose of this procedure is to identify employee training needs and to provide the training required to ensure quality of product and service, *awareness of significant environmental impacts, and prevention of pollution* and to satisfy the identified needs.

---

**2.0 Scope**

This procedure identifies the training and development opportunities provided to all Mega Manufacturing employees. It outlines the structured program which has been established to ensure program development, training, and evaluation for all Mega Manufacturing employees whose work affects quality.

---

As written, the scope is as appropriate to an environmental management system as to a quality assurance system. The only limiting factor is the focus on employees whose work affects quality. For an integrated procedure, the last line should be revised as:

. . . employees whose work affects quality *and/or the environment.*

---

**3.0 Definitions/Acronyms**

   3.1   OJT   On-the-Job Training
   3.2   STS   Specialty Training Standard

**4.0 References**

   4.1   ISO 9002, Paragraph 4.18

---

Reference to ISO 14001, Paragraph 4.4.2 should be added.

---

**5.0 Procedure**

   5.1   Training needs or recertification requirements for all Mega Manufacturing personnel are identified by production managers, supervisors, executive staff members, or the training manager.

      5.1.1   Training that is related to tasks associated with quality of product and service is recorded on the employee's Specialty Training Standard form.

No revision is required in Step 5.1 because training needs and recertification are not linked specifically to quality. As written, the statement applies equally to ISO 14001. However, Step 5.1.1 indicates that only training needs related to quality are to be recorded. For consistency with the purpose and scope of this procedure, Step 5.1.1 should be revised to read:

> Training that is related to tasks associated with quality of product and service and/or *significant environmental impacts* are recorded on the employee's Specialty Training Standard form.

As revised, Step 5.1.1 addresses employees whose work may create a significant environmental impact, but it does not address the requirement for awareness training. A new step, 5.1.2, can be added:

> 5.1.2    *Training that is related to awareness of environmental man-agement, the effects of environmental management on each area and job function, and the potential consequences of departure from established operating procedures is recorded on the employee's Specialty Training Standard form.*

Steps 5.2 and 5.3 describe roles and responsibilities related to the location of training rather than the substance of that training. As written, they apply equally to training conducted in support of quality assurance and environmental management. Therefore, no revisions are necessary. Nor is any revision required for Steps 5.4 through 5.8 because all statements apply equally to quality and environmental recertification, scheduling, testing, and so forth. (The revised procedure is reproduced in its entirety immediately following this discussion.)

---

*6.0 Forms, Reports, and Quality Records*

| Name | Location | Retention |
|---|---|---|
| OJT Record (AT-QUL-17) | Training Mgr's office | Indefinite |
| Attendance sheet (AT-QUL-88) | Training Mgr's office | Indefinite |
| Specialty Training Standard | Training Mgr's office | Indefinite |
| Course tests | Training Mgr's office | Indefinite |

The heading should be revised to read *Forms, Reports, and Records,* because information now reflects an integrated system rather than just the quality system.

The revised procedure is

| Mega Manufacturing Procedure | | Procedure No.: | 40.180 |
|---|---|---|---|
| Subject: | Control of Training | Page: | 1 of 4 |
| | | Revision: | 1 |
| | | Effective Date: | Sep 15, 1998 |
| Prepared by: | Tom Traynor | Approved by: | Philip Forrest |
| | Training Manager | | Director, Human Resources |
| Date: | Aug 1, 1998 | Date: | Sep 1, 1998 |

1.0   Purpose

The purpose of this procedure is to identify employee training needs and to provide the training required to ensure quality of product and service, awareness of significant environmental impacts, and prevention of pollution and to satisfy the identified needs.

2.0   Scope

This procedure identifies the training and development opportunities provided to all Mega Manufacturing employees. It outlines the structured program which has been established to ensure program development, training, and evaluation for all Mega Manufacturing employees whose work affects quality and/or the environment.

3.0   Definitions/Acronyms

3.1   OJT  On-the-Job Training

3.2   STS  Specialty Training Standard

4.0   References

4.1   ISO 9002, Paragraph 4.18

4.2   ISO 14001, Paragraph 4.4.2

5.0  Procedure

    5.1  Training needs or recertification requirements for all Mega Manufacturing personnel are identified by production managers, supervisors, executive staff members, or the training manager.

        5.1.1  Training that is related to tasks associated with quality of product and service and/or significant environmental impacts is recorded on the employee's Specialty Training Standard form.

        5.1.2  Training that is related to awareness of environmental management, the effects of environmental management on each area and job function, and the potential consequences of departure from established operating procedures is recorded on the employee's Specialty Training Standard form.

    5.2  On-the-job training is conducted by the employee's supervisor/manager or another employee, designated by the supervisor/manager, who is qualified at least one skill level higher than the employee being trained.

        5.2.1  Training is recorded on OJT Records Form AT-QUL-17.

        5.2.2  OJT Records Form is sent to the training manager for inclusion in the employee's training file.

    5.3  If training is conducted at an off-base site, the training manager arranges registration for the trainee and coordinates hotel and travel arrangements through the Mega Manufacturing executive secretary.

        5.3.1  Training certificates or other evidence of training are retained by the trainee.

        5.3.2  A copy of the training certificate or other evidence is submitted to the training manager for inclusion in the employee's training file.

| Procedure #40.180-Control of Training | Revision: 1 | Page 3 of 4 |

5.4 When recertification or other formal training requirements are identified, the training manager determines whether the training expertise is available within Mega Manufacturing.

    5.4.1 If there is no internal source available, the training manager contacts a qualified subcontractor who can provide the required training and recertification. A verbal or written contract is initiated and a purchase order is prepared.

    5.4.2 If there is an internal source available, that individual is notified of the training requirement and his/her agreement to conduct the training is obtained by the training manager.

5.5 The training manager schedules the required training and notifies the attendee(s) of the scheduled class.

5.6 Training is conducted.

    5.6.1 If testing is conducted, the trainer grades each attendee's test and determines if he/she passed or failed.

    5.6.2 If an employee fails a test, he/she will be rescheduled for a subsequent training session.

5.7 At the conclusion of a training session, the attendance sheet (Form AT-QUL-88) is circulated through the class and returned to the trainer.

    5.7.1 An employee who does not attend a scheduled training session is rescheduled by the training manager and his/her supervisor is notified of the nonattendance.

5.8 The employee's training record is updated by the training manager. A copy of the attendance sheet and the course test, if one is conducted, are placed in the employee's training file.

| Procedure #40.180–Control of Training | Revision: 1 | Page 4 of 4 |

6.0   Forms, Reports, and Records

| Name | Location | Retention |
|------|----------|-----------|
| OJT Record (AT-QUL-17) | Training Mgr's office | Indefinite |
| Attendance sheet (AT-QUL-88) | Training Mgr's office | Indefinite |
| Specialty Training Standard | Training Mgr's office | Indefinite |
| Course tests | Training Mgr's office | Indefinite |

# CHAPTER 6

## Internal System Audits

Both ISO 9001/2 and ISO 14001 require that an organization periodically audit its system to verify its conformance to stated requirements in the relevant standard. This chapter discusses how internal quality management system (QMS) and environmental management system (EMS) audits should be conducted and what special considerations must be brought to bear when auditing an integrated system.

In order to understand how to effectively audit an integrated management system, it is important to understand what an audit is. ISO 8402, Quality management and quality assurance—Vocabulary, and ISO 10011, Guidelines for Auditing Quality Systems, define a quality audit as a

> Systematic and independent examination to determine whether quality activities and related results comply with planned arrangements and whether these arrangements are implemented effectively and are suitable to achieve objectives.

ISO 14010, Guidelines for environmental auditing—General principles, similarly defines an environmental audit as a

> Systematic, documented verification process of objectively obtaining and evaluating audit evidence to determine whether specified environmental activities, events, conditions, management systems, or information about these matters conform with audit criteria, and communicating the results of this process to the client.

ISO 14010 was written to apply to all kinds of environmental audits, including regulatory compliance audits. ISO 14011, Guidelines for environmental auditing—Auditing of environmental management systems, narrows the definition of an EMS audit:

77

Systematic, documented verification process of objectively obtaining and evaluating audit evidence to determine whether an organization's environmental management system conforms to the environmental management system audit criteria, and communicating the results of this process to the client.

The definitions of QMS and EMS audits are similar. Both emphasize a systematic, unbiased assessment to determine whether the system in question meets all requirements imposed by its guiding standard. As discussed in chapter 2, ISO 9001/2 and ISO 14001 contain a number of similar requirements. Differences in auditing the two systems typically reflect auditor background and experience rather than significant differences in the standards. Auditors with experience in environmental regulatory compliance audits sometimes find it difficult to separate compliance issues from system concepts. Auditors from the quality arena tend to have difficulty auditing a system that is not required to document all procedures. However, the audit process is the same for a stand-alone ISO 9001/2 system, a stand-alone ISO 14001 system, or an integrated ISO 9001/2-14001 system.

## THE AUDIT CYCLE

An internal systems audit should provide objective evidence that the implemented system conforms with all requirements of the guiding standard and any additional requirements that the organization has imposed upon itself. The audit cycle includes four sets of activities that assure collection of information necessary for evaluating the effectiveness of the implemented system—planning the audit, conducting the audit, reporting, and follow-up.

### Planning the Audit

The first planning task requires establishing an audit schedule. ISO 9001/2 requires that internal quality audits are conducted "on the basis of the status and importance of the activity to be audited," while ISO 14001 states that EMS audits will be conducted periodically and the schedule based on "the environmental importance of the activity concerned and the results of previous audits." Because no time period is mandated by either standard, scheduling is at the discretion of the organization.

Most companies with mature systems employ an internal audit schedule that reflects the schedule followed by their registrars. Once a registration audit has been conducted and a company is registered, a surveillance audit is conducted approximately every six months. Typically at the end of three years, a reregistration audit is conducted.

The size and complexity of a company will determine whether an internal surveillance audit is deemed necessary quarterly, semiannually or annually. Depending on the resources available, it may be more efficient to conduct a larger number of surveillance audits (e.g., four/year) that examine only a few elements of the system each time and can be done quickly or a smaller number (e.g., two/year) that look at more elements of the system and require more person-days.

The second planning task entails a document review (sometimes called a *desktop* review because material is usually evaluated in the auditor's office rather than on the facility floor). The document review is an assessment of the organization's manual (in the case of ISO 9001/2 or an integrated system) or other description of the system's core elements (in the case of ISO 14001), procedures, and work instructions. The purpose of this review is to determine whether all required procedures have been developed and adequately fulfill their intended purpose.

ISO 9001/2 requires that all procedures are documented (i.e., written). If a required procedure has not been developed, it becomes evident during the document review and the auditor can judge whether the on-site conformity assessment is warranted.

ISO 14001 poses a greater challenge. Most of the required procedures do not have to be documented. There are only three references to documented procedures in the entire standard—operational control (section 4.4.6a), monitoring and measuring key characteristics of operations and activities with significant environmental aspects (4.5.1, first paragraph), and evaluating compliance with relevant environmental legislation and regulations (4.5.1, third paragraph). This means that the document review cannot be used as a screen for determining whether to proceed with the rest of the audit. The absence of documented procedures does not necessarily mean there has been a failure to establish and implement procedures.

In an integrated system, all procedures must be documented. Wherever there are differences between the quality and environmental management standards, a company must conform to the more stringent requirement. Because ISO 9001/2 requires documented procedures, an integrated system must be documented or it will not be in conformance with the quality standard.

There are many different approaches to performing the document review. The authors' experience suggests that using a matrix saves valuable time and generates good results.

The matrix approach identifies the requirements of the standard of interest (or both standards in an integrated system) down the left column. The top row identifies categories of documents (i.e., manual, procedures, work instructions, forms, and records). Every requirement that is addressed is noted in the appropriate cell. Blank cells indicate seemingly missing elements of the system and determine where additional investigation is needed. Figure 6.1 provides an example of a documentation review matrix. Once the document review is completed, the auditor must determine the makeup of the audit team, create the checklists that will be used, and design the audit plan.

The structure of the audit team is an important element in any audit. In an integrated systems audit, it is crucial to have auditors who understand both standards (ISO 9001/2 and ISO 14001) and the similarities between them. If it is not possible to work with individual auditors who have such experience, the next best approach is to establish an audit team composed of auditors from each of the systems. Obviously, knowledge of the standards alone is insufficient—auditors must be properly trained in auditing techniques.

The key to a good audit is the checklist, a tool that contains questions about the system, the relationship between the questions and specific requirements in the guiding standards, and methods for verifying the answers to those questions. A well-designed checklist helps assure that the audit is effective.

The types and forms of checklists are as varied as the number of activities audited in an organization. Virtually any format is acceptable as long as it meets the needs of the audit process, reflects auditee requirements, and covers the audited area. A well-constructed checklist will

- Address every audit activity separately. ISO 9001 contains 20 clauses, many with subclauses; ISO 9002 contains 19; and ISO 14001, 17. Each clause must be evaluated. In a single-system audit, it is common to develop the checklist by working through the standard in chronological order. In an

| Requirement (ISO 9001-ISO 14001) | Manual | Procedure | Instruction | Form/Record |
|---|---|---|---|---|
| Management Responsibility (4.1/4.4.1) | | | | |
| Quality policy (4.1.1/) | p. 4 | | | |
| Environmental policy (/4.2) | p. 5 | | | |
| Communication of policies (4.1.1/4.2e) | | #15-412 | | |
| Responsibility and authority (4.1.2.1/4.4.1) | pp. 7-9 | | | #QF-3-17 |
| a) prevent nonconformities (4.1.2.1) | p. 7 | | | |
| b) identify and record problems (4.1.2.1) | p.7 | | | |
| c) initiate solutions (4.1.2.1) | p. 8 | | | |
| d) verify implementation of solutions (4.1.2.1) | p. 8 | | | |
| e) control nonconforming product (4.1.2.1) | p. 9 | | | |
| Resources (4.1.2.2/4.4.1) | p. 14 | | | 98 budget |
| Management representative (4.1.2.3/4.4.1) | p. 7 | | | |
| Management review (4.1.3/4.6) | p. 15 | #15-501 | | meeting minutes |
| Continue with remaining requirements | | | | |

Figure 6.1  Documentation Review Matrix

integrated system audit, however, it is imperative to develop a checklist that captures the combined set of elements.

- Provide a way to reference the specific requirement being examined. A single numbered clause or subclause can contain more than one requirement (designated by the verb *shall*). Therefore, reference to the specific *shall* under review is essential. The authors' experience suggests reproducing the actual requirement on the checklist to avoid confusion or misinterpretation.

- Identify where in the standard, manual, or documented procedure the specific requirement is specified. Most checklist questions will be based on requirements that appear in the guiding standard. However, companies often impose additional requirements upon themselves. These typically appear in the system manual or documented procedures. The checklist should identify the source and location of the requirement under review (e.g., ISO 14001, 4.4.6c; or EMS manual, section 5.2; or quality system procedure #30-12, rev. 3).

- Delineate how conformance will be assessed. This point is critical and differentiates an effective checklist from an interview protocol. It is insufficient to accept the answers to questions at face value. The auditor must verify system conformance by looking at objective evidence. For every question asked, there must be some form of objective evidence that will be used to verify conformance or corroborate a finding of nonconformance.

  It is important to remember that objective evidence is not always in the form of written records. It also includes interview data (what better way to verify that employees understand the company policy than to ask them to explain it) and observation of activities (if a procedure specifies that round widgets always get placed in a red box and square widgets in a yellow box, watching widget sorters may be the best way to establish whether the procedure is being followed).

- Allow space for recording and explaining any observations. Developing a good checklist requires time and effort. Before marking it up with notes, be sure to retain a clean master copy for use in subsequent audits.

An example of a typical checklist page is presented in Figure 6.2. The checklist is a valuable tool, but in and of itself cannot guarantee a successful audit. How the auditor asks the questions on the checklist is as important as the questions that are asked. (Questioning techniques are discussed later in this chapter.) Because the internal audit team is going to ask the questions, audit team members should participate in their development. If checklist questions are developed by the lead auditor, audit team members should have an opportunity to review the checklist to be sure that they understand the purpose of each requirement, intent of each question, and method of verification. Using a group of unfamiliar questions will hinder an auditor's ability to gain the in-depth knowledge necessary for a successful audit.

The third key element in planning entails creating an audit plan. The audit plan must be designed for the specific audit that is being conducted. It lays out how the audit will be conducted, but must be flexible in order to allow for changes in approach caused by the information that is gathered during the audit. A typical audit plan includes

- Audit objectives and scope
- Audit criteria
- Functional areas, persons, or organizations to be audited
- Expected time and duration of significant audit activities
- Dates and locations of audit and related meetings
- Names of audit team members

There are many ways to prepare an audit plan. One of the most common is a chart. Quality auditors tend to organize such charts by functional area within the facility to be audited (e.g., shipping department, quality lab). EMS auditors tend to organize their charts by elements in the ISO 14001 (e.g., training, legal requirements). Neither approach is inherently better than the other. For an integrated audit, the authors' experience suggests that organizing the plan by elements is more efficient. However, auditors should select whatever approach best suits them. The first page of a typical audit plan is presented in Figure 6.3. The plan depicted in Figure 6.3 is designed to be realistic and flexible. It allows 15 minutes between interviews. This gives the auditors time to enhance notes, attend to personal needs, and get from one location to the next.

| AUDIT CHECKLIST | Rev. No. _____ |
|---|---|
| | Eff. Date _____ |

**Requirement:**

| Questions: | Verification: |
|---|---|
| | |

**Notes:**

| Organization audited: | Area audited: |
|---|---|
| Contact: | Audit date: |
| Auditor: | |

**Figure 6.2**   Checklist Form

| Objective: | Determine system conformance | Auditee: | Mega Manufacturing |
| Scope: | Big City, NM facility | Auditee contact: | S. Mann |
| Criteria: | ISO 9001 and ISO 14001 | Auditors: | P&B Company |
| Schedule | | | |

| Schedule | Lead Auditor P. White | Auditor J. Olsen | Auditor L. Lane |
| --- | --- | --- | --- |
| 25 July 98 | Lead Auditor P. White | Auditor J. Olsen | Auditor L. Lane |
| 8:00–8:30 | Opening meeting | Opening meeting | Opening meeting |
| 8:45–9:45 | John Smith, VP (mgt. responsibility and authority) | Irma Riddler, Atty. (laws/regulations) | David Jones, Mgr. (training) |
| 10:00–11:00 | Ken Johnson, Mgr. (audit program) | Carol Baker, Mgr. (inspection and testing) | Larry Silver, VP (purchasing) |
| 11:15–12:15 | Ed Burke, Eng. (process controls) | Joe Green, Eng. (env. aspects and impacts) | Susan Green, Mgr. (internal communications) |
| 12:15–1:00 | Lunch | Lunch | Lunch |
| 1:15–2:15 | M. Freeze, Mgr. (calibration) | J. Glenn, Eng. (process control) | Robert Hall, VP (external communications) |
| 2:30–3:30 | Joe Joker, VP (contract review) | Alice White, Mgr. (documentation) | Jim Dayton, Mgr. (records) |
| 3:45–4:30 | Audit team meeting | Audit team meeting | Audit team meeting |
| 4:45–5:15 | Debriefing | Debriefing | Debriefing |

| | | |
| --- | --- | --- |
| Opening meeting: | July 25 | 8:00–8:30 A.M. |
| Debriefings: | July 25, 26, 27 | 4:45–5:15 P.M. |
| 2nd shift observations: | July 26 | 6:00–10:00 P.M. |
| Closing meeting: | July 28 | 2:00–3:30 P.M. |

Prepared by: P. White, Lead Auditor, July 7, 1998

Approved by: S. Mann, Facility Manager, July 8, 1998

**Figure 6.3** First Page of Audit Plan for Integrated ISO 9001- ISO 14001 Management System

The fourth and final task in the audit planning phase is notification. The audit schedule referred to at the beginning of this chapter typically identifies the quarter or month in which an audit will occur. The auditee should be contacted in person or by telephone to establish specific audit dates within that scheduled time frame. This also is an opportunity to discuss the scope and objectives of the audit. Once the dates are agreed, the auditor should put all information in writing and send a copy to the auditee as confirmation.

Some auditors, particularly those with a background in regulatory compliance, insist that audits should not be announced in advance. Their feeling is that auditing without any advance warning allows auditors to find problems before the auditee has time to correct them. In a systems audit, however, the overall objective is to verify that the auditee has implemented and is following all necessary procedures. If the act of notification causes the auditee to implement and follow proper procedures, the objective of the audit has been met.

### Conducting the Audit

Four tasks are involved in conducting the audit—opening meeting, collecting objective evidence, debriefing meetings, and closing meeting.

### Opening Meeting

In a registration audit, the opening meeting is a critical activity because, in many cases, this is the first time that the audit team and the auditee meet face-to-face. This is the lead auditor's only opportunity to make a good first impression (in real life, there are no do-overs) so preparation is essential. In an internal audit, the opening meeting is necessary to begin the process, but typically is less formal.

The opening meeting is chaired by the lead auditor and attended by all audit team members and senior management of the organization, department, or facility to be audited. The lead auditor must ensure that the audit team and all auditee representatives understand and agree to all pertinent details of the audit. Therefore, the lead auditor must introduce audit team members and meet their auditee counterparts, confirm the audit scope, present the audit plan, discuss audit sequence, confirm plans for debriefings and the closing meeting, and establish channels of communication. The lead auditor should emphasize that the audit is not an *I gotcha* exercise; rather, it

| | |
|---|---|
| 8:00–8:05 | Introductions |
| 8:05–8:10 | Audit scope and criteria |
| 8:10–8:20 | Audit plan review |
| | • how audit will be conducted |
| | • auditee responsibilities if nonconformances are identified |
| 8:20–8:25 | Confirmation of scheduled activities |
| | • interviews |
| | • debriefings |
| | • closing meeting |
| 8:25–8:30 | Communication channels |

**Figure 6.4**   Opening Meeting Agenda

is a constructive activity for the betterment of the system. Figure 6.4 illustrates an opening meeting agenda.

The opening meeting should not present new information to the auditee. It is intended to confirm what has already been agreed to during audit preparation and provide the opportunity to modify the audit plan if unforeseen circumstances at the auditee's facility so require. With proper preparation, the opening meeting should take only 20 to 30 minutes.

Internal auditors often view an opening meeting as unnecessary. After all, they are auditing an organization, department, or facility with which they are highly familiar. No matter how well an auditor knows the auditee, the opening meeting is an important element in assuring that the audit runs smoothly. It is a time to make sure that there are no misunderstandings about any portion of the audit process.

### Collecting Objective Evidence

Objective evidence must be collected if the auditor is to assess whether an organization's management system conforms to stated requirements in the guiding standard. Such evidence takes several forms—examination of documents and records, observation, and interview. Typically, quality auditors spend much of their time observing different activities and comparing them to documented procedures. However, this approach may be less fruitful for EMS auditors because few procedures required by ISO 14001 have to be documented. EMS auditors typically spend much of their time interviewing workers throughout the organization to elicit information concerning established procedures prior to observing whether such procedures are being followed.

In a fully integrated system, all procedures must be documented or the system will not conform to the quality standard, which specifies written documentation. In a partially integrated system, all procedures that are common to both systems (see Figure 5.1) must be documented to conform with quality requirements. However, any procedures that are unique to the environmental management system do not have to be documented unless ISO 14001 so states.

Because much of an EMS auditor's time is spent interviewing workers throughout the auditee's organization, it is necessary to understand the basics of good interviewing techniques. A key factor in any interview process is the tendency to impute the motives of interviewees based on auditor impressions.

Sources of error that may affect an exchange of questions and answers and, therefore, auditor judgements based on the exchange include

- Semantic difference—dissimilar understanding of the meaning of words in a question or answer
- Contagious bias—process by which the views of the questioner are reflected in questions and influence the answers given by the interviewee
- Halo effect—positive interpretation of all interviewee responses as a result of good responses to initial questions
- Midpoint of series effect—interviewee responses are interpreted as moderate or average rather than more disparate or extreme

These sources of interviewer error are greatly minimized by the use of checklists. Written questions guide the auditor through an interview. Although checklist questions are seldom asked verbatim, they keep the interview focused because the auditor is responsible for obtaining answers that are meaningful. *Tell me! Show me!* should be the bywords of every audit. Verification of all information obtained during interviews discourages the interviewee from not providing the auditor with factual information and prevents the auditor from mis-interpreting what has been conveyed.

Other tips that enhance the interview process are

- Ask open-ended questions—who, what, when, where, why, how?—to elicit information. "Yes/no" questions are appropriate in some instances, but often fail to yield the kind of information needed to assess conformance.

- Ask the same question several times of different people. This enables the auditor to judge whether he/she is getting the *real* answer.

- Separate levels of supervision when asking questions. This is more likely to result in full disclosure rather than a carefully edited version designed to keep the interviewee's boss happy.

- Go beyond the scope of written questions based on an interviewee's responses. Dig deeper into problem areas and don't hesitate to follow your nose.

- Don't constantly ask questions. Some answers are best obtained by silent observation.

The key to a good interview is the auditor's ability to listen. The process of accurately understanding another individual's viewpoint requires the suspension of judgements at the time of the interview. Arguing or overly encouraging an interviewee exerts a degree of influence that may taint the information that is being gathered. Auditor responses during an interview should be neu-tral—there will be ample opportunity to express judgements later in the audit.

During the audit process, it is critical to take good notes as these will be used to prepare nonconformance reports for use at the clos-ing meeting and in writing the audit report. There is no single format for summarizing and reporting the results of an audit. Figure 6.5 contains a format that the authors find useful.

Every nonconformance report (NCR) developed during an audit should be uniquely numbered. The type of nonconformance (major or minor), necessary in a registration audit, is optional for internal audits. Some companies prefer to differentiate major and minor non-conformances because this information helps the auditee allocate resources for corrective and preventive action. Others believe that

| NONCONFORMANCE REPORT | Audit No. _____ |
|---|---|
| | Note No. _____ |
| **Auditee:** Name of company and facility being audited | |
| **Area Audited:** Department, section, or area within facility (e.g., receiving, purchasing, shipping) | |
| **Requirement:** Specific requirement that is violated | |
| **Nonconformance:**          *(Select category)*   ☐ Major     ☐ Minor<br><br>Description of the nonconformance and categorization as either major or minor | |
| **Objective Evidence:**<br><br>Specific instances of infractions | |
| Auditor: | Date: |

**Figure 6.5**   Nonconformance Report Form

designating a nonconformance as minor trivializes the need to correct and prevent the identified problem.

The NCR also provides space to identify the standard (e.g., ISO
9002) and requirement (e.g., 4.18) to which the nonconformance is
related. In an integrated system, the auditor may find it necessary to
identify both standards and the requirement numbers of each, where
those requirements overlap. The source of additional requirements
that a company has imposed upon itself also should be referenced
here (e.g., System Manual, section 5.3).

Some organizations also note observations on the NCR. An
observation is *not* a nonconformance. Rather, it is a poor management practice that could eventually result in a nonconformance.
Internal auditors frequently focus on observations with the same
intensity as nonconformances in an effort to improve the system on
a continual basis.

Clarity and precision are important requirements for any report.
For quality and environmental management system nonconformances, they are vital. Any identified nonconformance must be
linked to an explicit requirement in the guiding standard. Moreover,
the objective evidence that *proves* the nonconformance must be
clearly articulated. It is insufficient for an auditor to intuit or feel
that a requirement is not being met. If the auditor cannot identify the
evidence that supports a finding of nonconformance, he/she probably has not identified a nonconformance. Figures 6.6 and 6.7 illustrate unsatisfactory and satisfactory ways of completing the NCR.

There are two things wrong with the report shown in Figure 6.6.
First, it does not actually state the nonconformance. It presents the
objective evidence twice. Second, the objective evidence is presented
in vague terms, making it difficult for the auditee to understand the
deficiency that has to be corrected and prevented in the future.

Figure 6.7 illustrates a more satisfactory record. The distinction
between the nonconformance and supporting evidence is laid out
clearly and precisely. Note that ISO 14001, clause 4.5.1, requires
only *calibration,* but that the auditee's own procedure G-23 specifies
calibration interval.

Note also gauge #ZXX-095. It was calibrated within the prescribed interval. However, it violates clause 4.5.1 because the auditee's own G-23 requires a sticker to indicate the calibration status.
(ISO 14001 requires that "records of this process shall be retained

| NONCONFORMANCE REPORT | Audit No. ___98/02___ |
|---|---|
| | Note No. ____1____ |
| Auditee: Mega Manufacturing | |
| Area Audited:  Production | |
| Requirement: ISO 9001, clause 4.11.1—Establish and maintain documented procedures to control, calibrate, and maintain inspection, measuring, and test equipment.<br><br>ISO 14001, clause 4.5.1—Monitoring equipment shall be calibrated and maintained according to the organization's procedures. | |
| Nonconformance:              *(Select category)*  ■ Major     □ Minor<br><br>Gauges in the production area were past their calibration due dates. | |
| Objective Evidence:<br><br><br>Several gauges in the production area had stickers with expired dates on them. | |
| Auditor:    P. White | Date:    July 25, 1998 |

**Figure 6.6**   Nonconformance Report Form

| NONCONFORMANCE REPORT | Audit No. ___98/02___ |
| --- | --- |
| | Note No. ____2____ |

**Auditee:** Mega Manufacturing

**Area Audited:** Production

**Requirement:** ISO 9001, clause 4.11.1 and ISO 14001, clause 4.5.1— Calibration of equipment used for inspection, monitoring, measuring, and testing

**Nonconformance:**          *(Select category)*   ◼ Major    ☐ Minor

Inspection and test equipment is not being calibrated within the intervals prescribed in Mega Manufacturing Procedure G-23.

**Objective Evidence:**

Ten gauges were selected at random from the production area and the sticker required by G-23 was checked. Those with expired stickers were compared against the calibration database. Gauge numbers and status were:

| | |
| --- | --- |
| ZPG-009: ok | BBK-012: exp. sticker, no cal record |
| BBK-104: ok | ZXX-095: exp. sticker, cal record exists |
| ASD-518: exp. sticker, no cal record | |
| | ZPG-016: exp. sticker, no cal record |
| RTF-002: ok | BBJ-005: exp. sticker, no cal record |
| ZXX-064: ok | RTF-021: ok |

Five of the 10 gauges had expired stickers. One of those had been calibrated without being restickered. No calibration evidence for the others could be located.

| Auditor:   P. White | Date:   July 25, 1998 |
| --- | --- |

**Figure 6.7**   Nonconformance Report Form

according to the organization's procedures.") Alternatively, gauge #ZXX-095 could be recorded on a separate NCR because it violates a different requirement.

In this example, the auditor dug deeper with follow-up questions. After finding the expired stickers, the auditor located the actual calibration records. An expired sticker does not necessarily mean that an instrument has not been calibrated; it means only that the sticker has not been updated. Based on the sticker alone, it would be premature to make judgements about calibration status.

### Debriefing Meetings

Observations and alleged nonconformances should be discussed with the auditee's management team on a daily basis. This accomplishes two important tasks. First, it alerts management to seeming deficiencies in the system so there are no surprises in the closing meeting. Second, it provides the audit team with an important sanity check. If additional information related to a seeming nonconformance exists within the company, the audit team can be alerted and extend its inquiry to be sure that all pertinent data have been examined. Until the audit team conducts the closing meeting, it should continue to collect sufficient objective evidence for making informed judgements and drawing appropriate conclusions. Debriefings provide an excellent opportunity for this.

### The Closing Meeting

When the audit is complete, the audit team conducts a closing meeting to formally present any nonconformances identified and clarify any misunderstandings. The content and presentation of this meeting are critical to the success of the audit. Therefore, the lead auditor must be fully prepared to address all areas covered during the audit.

Preparation is the key to assure that the closing meeting runs smoothly and effectively. During the audit, auditors should take extensive notes and develop nonconformance reports. To ensure that nothing is missed, the lead auditor should prepare an audit summary that identifies the status of every requirement in the guiding standard. An audit status summary form is presented in Figure 6.8. The summary form is straightforward when doing either a QMS or EMS audit. For an integrated audit, the summary form requires some

| Requirement (9001/14001) | OK | NA | Nonconformances | Systemic? |
|---|---|---|---|---|
| Quality policy (4.1.1/) | ✔ | | | Y☐ N☐ |
| Environmental policy (/4.2) | ✔ | | | Y☐ N☐ |
| Organization (4.1.2/4.4.1) | ✔ | | | Y☐ N☐ |
| Management review (4.1.3/4.6) | | | Designated mgt rep not identified | Y☒ N☐ |

**Figure 6.8** Audit Status Summary Form

manipulation to ensure that all overlapping quality and environmental requirements are captured despite different numbering sequences.

Planning the meeting is especially challenging, considering the short amount of time allowed for its preparation after completion of the physical audit. To assure maximum impact, the lead auditor may want to use visual aids or hand out copies of the NCRs. It may also be beneficial to have different audit team members present various sections, especially if the audit was complex because of the size of the organization and the scope of quality and environmental responsibilities.

The lead auditor should clearly understand the meeting's objectives, which include

- Assuring that the auditee understands the significance of the nonconformances and the need for corrective action
- Providing the auditee an opportunity to explain any unusual or discrepant information obtained during the audit
- Providing the audit team an opportunity to demonstrate to the auditee the validity of all nonconformances

If the audit was properly conducted, there should be no surprises to the auditee. All information presented should have been discussed with auditee management during the audit. Even so, it is courteous for the lead auditor to meet briefly with the most senior management representative just prior to the closing meeting to summarize the content and format of the meeting.

Conducting a constructive closing meeting requires the skilled leadership of the lead auditor, who must continually stress that the audit team's priority is to assist the auditee in pursuing an effective management system. Above all, the lead auditor must maintain positive control throughout the meeting. Positive thinking by the lead auditor will promote positive thinking by the auditee.

The meeting should be conducted so as to leave no loose ends regarding nonconformances. The auditee must be made to understand the need for corrective action and a date for submission of a corrective action plan should be mutually agreed.

Finally, the lead auditor should point out that the final audit report will be issued as an official record of the management system audit.

### Audit Report

The lead auditor is responsible for preparing the audit report which becomes the official record of the audit. The lead auditor must be sure that the report accurately reflects audit findings and conclusions. The report will indicate whether the management system conforms with all requirements and if it has been properly implemented and maintained.

The audit report should be compiled, written, and submitted as soon as possible to enable the auditee to begin necessary corrective action. Typically, audit reports are submitted no later than 10 working days after the closing meeting.

An audit report should include

- Background information—This section of the report describes the audit purpose, scope, and objectives. It lists the organization(s) audited, date and location of the audit, and auditees and auditors who participated in the audit. This section also contains approval authority for the report and applicable signatures.

- Executive summary—Key executives may not have time to read a full audit report. Without this section, audit findings may not receive necessary management attention and reaction. Key information items requiring action should be summarized clearly and succinctly. It should summarize the observed effectiveness of the system elements that were audited. It also should include a summary of nonconformances and agreed timing for submission of the corrective action plan.

• Identification of findings—The body of the report identifies nonconformances and supporting objective evidence. There are as many formats for this as there are auditors. The three most common formats are illustrated in Figures 6.9, 6.10, and 6.11.

The method shown in Figure 6.9 is effective when an organization is preparing for registration. It allows evaluation of the strengths and weaknesses of the system on a requirement by requirement basis and, therefore, pinpoints exactly where effort must be concentrated to improve the system.

---

*4.4.4 Environmental management system documentation*
The organization shall establish and maintain information, in paper or electronic form, to

a) describe the core elements of the management system and their interaction

b) provide direction to related documentation

Nonconformances
1. EMS documentation does not describe all core elements.

2. EMS documentation does not refer to related procedures.

Objective evidence
1. EMS manual does not describe management review or continual improvement of the EMS.

2. Procedure for evaluating regulatory compliance (#17-2-5) is not referenced in EMS manual section 5.1.

---

**Figure 6.9**  Reporting by Element

The method in Figure 6.10 is helpful when determining the type and extent of problems within specific departments or functional areas. The report is structured according to the area visited during the audit.

The format illustrated in Figure 6.11, although less frequently used, is effective when auditing an integrated system. The matrix

---

AUDIT AREA—PINION LAB

Requirements:

*4.9 Process Control (ISO 9001)*
The supplier shall identify and plan the production, installation, and servicing processes which directly affect quality and shall ensure that these processes are carried out under controlled conditions. Controlled conditions shall include the following:

(g) suitable maintenance of equipment to ensure continuing process capability.

Records shall be maintained for qualified processes.

*4.12 Inspection and Test Status (ISO 9001)*
The inspection and test status shall be identified by suitable means, which indicate the conformance or nonconformance of product with regard to inspection and tests performed. The identification of inspection and test status shall be maintenance, as defined in the quality plan and/or documented procedures, throughout production, installation, and servicing of the product to ensure that only product that has passed the required inspections and tests [or released under an authorized concession (see 4.13.2)] is dispatched, used, or installed.

*4.4.6 Operational Control (ISO 14001)*
The organization shall identify those operations and activities that are associated with the identified significant environmental aspects in line with its policy, objectives, and targets. The organization shall plan these activities, including maintenance, in order to ensure that they are carried out under specified conditions.

Nonconformances
1. Components are not properly controlled or identified as to status.
2. Maintenance records in log book and on equipment do not agree.
3. There is no formal procedure or instruction for the pinion production activity.
4. There is no formal procedure or instruction for storing used solvents prior to transport for disposal.

---

**Figure 6.10**   Reporting by Area Audited

Objective Evidence

Reagents were stored in glass cabinet in lab. The auditor examined containers of hydroxy isobutyric acid (100g containers), citric acid, exchange resin, sodium hydroxide, and phenolphthalein. None of the containers indicated a status (accept/reject). There was no indication of date of receipt, or expiration date.

The pure water system maintenance log book indicates last entry December 1992 for cartridge replacement. Markings on cartridge indicate cartridges were changed in December 1993. Oven OEL#114 has maintenance sticker without any information.

The responsible Lab Manager indicated that there is a lack of required procedure or instruction for the pinion production activity.

A review of the procedures and discussions with the responsible Health and Safety Manager indicated a lack of required procedures and/or instructions for storing used solvents.

**Figure 6.10**   *concluded*

helps the auditee quickly and easily understand the elements where there are weaknesses in the system.

Regardless of the report format selected, the audit report must contain a formal corrective action request (CAR) form for every identified nonconformance. CARs, typically appended to the audit report, contain all of the information that appears on the nonconformance report form. Additionally, a CAR delineates specific information that is to be provided by the auditee and space to indicate whether the nonconformance has been appropriately corrected (see Figure 6.12).

*Audit Completion*

The audit is complete when all activities in the audit plan have been concluded, including distribution of the audit report. The auditee is responsible for determining and initiating any corrective actions needed to deal with identified nonconformances.

Mega Manufacturing's internal quality audit procedure is presented. Changes to accommodate requirements imposed by ISO 14001, clause 4.5.4, EMS Audits, are *italicized*.

| ISO 9001 Requirement | ISO 14001 Requirement | Nonconformances | Objective Evidence |
|---|---|---|---|
| *4.1.3 Management Review* <br><br> The supplier's management with executive responsibility shall review the quality system at defined intervals sufficient to ensure its continuing suitability and effectiveness in satisfying the requirements of this American National Standard and the supplier's stated quality policy and objectives. Records of such reviews shall be maintained. | *4.6 Management Review* <br><br> The organization's top management shall, at intervals it determines, review the environmental management system to ensure it continuing suitability, adequacy, and effectiveness. The management review process shall ensure that the necessary information is collected to allow management to carry out this evaluation. This review shall be documented. | The management review process, described in section 4.3 of the systems manual, has not been implemented. | EHS VP and four managers who are responsible for performing the system review indicated that they have not conducted such reviews. |

Figure 6.11   Reporting by Matrix Format

| CORRECTIVE ACTION REQUEST | Audit No. _____ |
|---|---|
| | Note No. _____ |

**Auditee:** Name of company and facility being audited

**Area Audited:** Department, section, or area within facility (e.g., receiving, purchasing, shipping)

**Requirement:** Specific requirement that is violated

**Nonconformance:**            *(Select category)*   ☐ Major      ☐ Minor

Description of the nonconformance and categorization as either major or minor.

**Objective Evidence:**

Specific instances of infractions

**Corrective Action Request:** See reverse side.

| Auditor: | Date: |
|---|---|

**Figure 6.12**   Modified Nonconformance Report Form for Corrective Action Request *(continued)*

# CORRECTIVE ACTION REQUEST

The following information is to be completed for the nonconformance described on the reverse side of the form.

Immediate action to correct problem:

Interim action to correct problem:

Root cause of problem:

Corrective action:

Preventive action:

Date of full conformance:

Submitted by:                                          Date:

Reply is:        ☐ Satisfactory        This requirement will be re-audited
                                       ☐ date _____
                                       ☐ during next scheduled
                                          surveillance

                 ☐ Unsatisfactory     Resubmit plan per attached letter

Auditor:                                               Date:

Result of re-audit:        ☐        Nonconformance now closed
                           ☐        Nonconformance not closed—refer to
                                    NCR number _____

Auditor:                                               Date:

**Figure 6.12**    Corrective Action Request, Side Two

## MEGA MANUFACTURING CORPORATION

| Integrated System Procedure | Procedure #: 40.170 |
|---|---|
| Title: Control of Internal System Audits | Revision: 01 |
| Responsibility: VP, Quality Assurance | Effective Date: Jul 31, 1998 |
| | Page: 1 of 4 |

1.0 Purpose

The purpose of this procedure is to define a program to audit internal procedures and processes on a regular basis, in order to determine the effectiveness of the *Integrated Management System*.

2.0 Scope

This procedure applies to all Production activities and all other related activities covered by the Mega Manufacturing *Integrated Management* System as defined in the Procedures and Instructions Manual.

3.0 References

3.1 ISO 9002, Paragraph 4.17

*3.2 ISO 14001, Paragraph 4.5.4*

*3.3* Internal Audit Log

4.0 Procedure

4.1 The Vice President Quality Assurance (or his designee) creates an Internal Audit Log based on

4.1.1 Individual area requirements and trend analysis

4.1.2 Maximum one-year interval

4.1.3 Exceptional condition or deficiency

4.1.4 Customer feedback

4.1.5 Repeated quality discrepancies

*4.1.6 Repeated adverse environmental impacts*

4.2 The Vice President Quality Assurance (or his designee) reviews and updates the Internal Audit Log and identifies next audit requirements.

4.3   The Vice President Quality Assurance selects the Lead Auditor based on

    4.3.1   Qualification as internal lead auditor

    4.3.2   Knowledge or expertise related to area to be audited

    4.3.3   Work schedule availability

4.4   The Lead Auditor

    4.4.1   Develops the audit plan

    4.4.2   Assembles the audit team based on 4.3.2 and 4.3.3

    4.4.3   Reviews the procedures of the department to be audited

    4.4.4   Decides what areas within the department will be audited

    4.4.5   Determines specific audit assignments

4.5   The auditors develop an audit checklist.

4.6   The Lead Auditor conducts a pre–audit briefing to

    4.6.1   Notify department manager of areas to be audited

    4.6.2   Advise department manager of his/her responsibilities

    4.6.3   Discuss selection and use of guides

    4.6.4   Discuss final report

    4.6.5   Confirm date and time of post–audit briefing

4.7   The Department Manager ensures that records and documents are available and assigns resources.

4.8   The Lead Auditor and audit team conduct the audit using the formulated audit plan and checklist. All findings are recorded.

4.9   The Lead Auditor conducts a post–audit briefing to

    4.9.1   Report audit results

| Procedure 40.170 Internal *System* Audits | Revision: 01 | Page 3 of 4 |
| --- | --- | --- |

    4.9.2    Summarize areas needing corrective action

    4.9.3    Schedule follow-up audit, if required

4.10    The Lead Auditor prepares a final report based on audit results.

4.11    The Lead Auditor forwards the audit report to the department manager of the area audited, Management Representative, Vice President Quality Assurance, and Vice President Operations.

    4.11.1    The Management Representative adds the audit report to the next Management Review agenda.

    4.11.2    If nonconformances exist, the department manager prepares a corrective action plan and submits it to the Lead Auditor within 15 days of receiving the audit report.

    4.11.3    If Corrective Action Plan is not submitted within 15 days, the Lead Auditor issues a delinquent notice to the department manager, Management Representative, Vice President Quality Assurance, and Vice President Operations.

4.12    The Lead Auditor reviews the Corrective Action Plan and approves or disapproves the plan.

    4.12.1    If the plan is disapproved, the Lead Auditor issues an Unapproved Response Notice to the department manager, Management Representative, Vice President Quality Assurance, and Vice President Operations.

4.13    The Lead Auditor conducts a follow-up audit to ensure that corrective actions have been taken.

    4.13.1    If corrective action is acceptable, return to Step 4.2.

    4.13.2    If corrective action is not acceptable, go to Step 4.14.

| Procedure 40.170 Internal *System* Audits | Revision: 01 | Page 4 of 4 |

4.14   If a nonconformance previously noted is still evident, the Lead Auditor issues a Repeat Nonconformance Notice, distributes it per Step 4.11, and submits a copy to the President.

Notice that the purpose of the procedure has been broadened to encompass all environmental requirements imposed by ISO 14001. The steps in the procedure, however, remain virtually unchanged. The actions taken by the Vice President–Quality Assurance, lead auditor, and others are appropriate whether the audit covers a QMS, EMS, or integrated system.

# CHAPTER 7

## Management Review

Those individuals with executive responsibility—*senior* management in ISO 90001 parlance; *top* management in ISO 14001—are required to evaluate the system at regular intervals. Unlike system audits, which are tactical, management reviews are strategic. Their purpose is to ensure that the quality and environmental management systems continue to be suitable (that is, appropriate to stated requirements) and effective (capable of producing desired results).

ISO 14001 also requires that the environmental management system be reviewed for adequacy. In other words, the system must reflect changing legislation and regulations, changing concerns of interested parties, changing technology, and changing operations and activities of the organization.

The QMS review is tied to satisfying a company's stated quality policy and objectives. The EMS review is linked to continual improvement (required by the environmental policy) and resulting improvements in environmental performance.

Companies with partially integrated systems typically conduct two separate reviews. One review examines all elements of the QMS; the other focuses on elements of the EMS. With this approach, elements and supporting procedures common to both systems are reviewed twice. A fully integrated system is subject to a single management review that is comprehensive enough to accommodate all elements.

Interestingly, neither standard requires the organization to establish a procedure that guides the conduct of the review. Most companies, however, develop a management review procedure to ensure adherence to a schedule and consistency from one review to the next.

## CONDUCTING THE REVIEW

One of the first issues that must be resolved concerns responsibility related to the management review. In addition to senior-level managers charged with conducting the review, thought must be given to others in the organization who are expected to provide information that supports the review (e.g., system auditors). QMS reviews for company-wide systems typically involve the company's president, vice presidents for manufacturing and sales, and the most senior individual with quality assurance responsibility (vice president or director). A facility-level system is more likely to involve the facility manager and his/her direct reports for operations, sales, purchasing, and quality assurance.

EMS review teams have a slightly different composition. Individuals with sales and quality management responsibilities are unlikely to be involved, while the vice president (or manager) of environment, health, and safety (EHS) is an important participant.

Integrated system review teams tend to combine the two groups—those with quality and EHS responsibilities both participate.

The timing of reviews also must be considered. Many companies conduct an annual review of the system. Depending on the complexity of a company's processes, the review may take anywhere from a half day to a full day. The larger number of participants in an integrated review suggests that additional time will be required. For planning purposes, the authors find that activities related to an integrated system tend to require fifty percent more time than is needed for a stand-alone system. If a QMS or EMS review was conducted in a half day (four hours), an integrated review probably requires six hours.

Although the entire system needs to be reviewed, there is no requirement that a company must look at all elements at one time. Some companies review selected elements of the system each quarter so that the entire system is reviewed during the year. In fact, Annex A to ISO 14001, Guidance on the use of the specification, states that all elements of an environmental management system do not need to be reviewed at once and the review process may take place over a period of time.

The decision to review the entire system at once or break the review into pieces should be informed by the kind and amount of information that will be examined. Because ISO 9001/2 states that "the results of internal quality audits form an integral part of the input to management review activities" (Note 20), review teams often conclude that the only input for the management review process comes from internal audits.

Reviews should include results from system audits as well as information received from functional departments, customers, regulators, and the public. Functional departments can provide valuable information about performance measures and the extent to which stated objectives have been achieved. Information about customer satisfaction and servicing will contribute to evaluation of elements related to quality, while changing regulations, new technology, and concerns of interested parties will help determine whether planned arrangements for environmental concerns continue to be appropriate. The amount of information to be studied prior to the system review or presented at the review may dictate the wisdom of one complete evaluation versus several partial efforts.

Both standards require that this review is documented. Documentation can take any form deemed appropriate by the management review team. Typically, the review meeting agenda, attendance sheet, and minutes provide evidence that the review has occurred.

Mega Manufacturing's management review procedure is presented. Changes to accommodate requirements imposed by ISO 14001, clause 4.6, Management Review, are *italicized*.

## MEGA MANUFACTURING CORPORATION

| *Internal* System Procedure | Procedure #: 40.10 |
|---|---|
| Title: Management Review | Revision: *01* |
| Responsibility: VP, Quality Assurance | Effective Date: *Jul 31, 1998* |
| | Page: 1 of 3 |

1.0   Purpose

This procedure is designed to ensure that Mega Manufacturing management with executive responsibility review the company *integrated* system at defined intervals to ensure its continued stability and effectiveness in satisfying the requirements of ISO 9002 *and ISO 14001* as well as the Mega Manufacturing quality *and environmental* polic*ies* and objectives.

| Procedure 40.10 Management Review | Revision: *01* | Page 2 of 3 |

2.0  Scope

ISO 9002 requires a quality system be established, implemented, and maintained and that periodic reviews of the system be made by senior management as a basis for continuous improvement of the quality system.

*ISO 14001 requires an environmental management system be established, implemented, and maintained and that periodic reviews of the system be made by top management as a basis for continual improvement of the EMS in order to improve overall environmental performance.*

3.0  References

3.1  ISO 9002, Paragraph 4.1.3

*3.2  ISO 14001, Paragraph 4.6*

3.3  Corrective Action Plan Log (AT-AQL-91)

4.0  Procedure

4.1  The Management Representative schedules *system* review meetings at least quarterly and notifies all attendees of date, place, time, and expected duration.

4.2  The Management Representative prepares the meeting agenda to include

- Information from audit reports
- Open items from the Corrective Action Plan log
- Any items from the previous meeting that were not concluded
- Any items from the previous meeting that were added to the Corrective Action Plan log

4.3  The Management Representative conducts the meeting and assigns someone to take minutes.

4.3.1  Minutes of the previous meeting are reviewed and any corrections required are noted in the current minutes.

| Procedure 40.10 Management Review | Revision: *01* | Page 3 of 3 |
|---|---|---|

4.3.2  Reports on quality *and environmental* issues are given, as required, by various team leaders and department managers.

4.3.3  The *System* Auditor discusses nonconformances or potential problems discovered in recent audits.

4.3.4  The Engineering Manager reports on any recent test cell rejects and reviews probable causes for rejects.

*4.3.5  The EHS Manager reports on any recent changes in regulatory requirements and/or the views of external interested parties.*

4.3.6  The *System* Review Team Leader reports on issues currently under investigation or on ones that have been closed or turned into corrective action requests (CARs) since the last *System* Review meeting.

4.3.7  A Quality Assurance Department representative *and an EHS Department representative* review all outstanding CARs not addressed by the *System Review* Team Leader.

4.4  The Management Representative assigns to attendees any research tasks or special projects to be investigated and reported on at the next meeting.

4.5  The Management Representative concludes the meeting when all reports and projects are completed.

4.6  The Minutes Taker prepares the minutes of the meeting and submits them to the Management Representative for review and approval.

4.7  When the minutes are approved, the Minutes Taker makes copies and distributes them to all attendees.

As with other ISO 9002 procedures at Mega Manufacturing, the purpose has been broadened to capture the intent of ISO 14001 while the procedure itself has been modified only slightly.

## IMPLEMENTING MANAGEMENT REVIEW DECISIONS

A comprehensive review of the QMS, EMS, or integrated system in and of itself does not fully conform to this requirement. Conclusions and recommendations are intended to provide the basis for necessary action to improve the system. Auditors will not limit their investigation to verifying that the management review has been documented; they will also look to see whether responsibility has been assigned, activities initiated, and progress evaluated for all identified system improvements.

Companies typically handle EMS improvements in one of two ways. Some organizations use the *corrective action request* model. This approach captures a single issue targeted for improvement on a system improvement form (similar to a corrective action request) and asks the responsible individual to develop a plan for strengthening the system.

Alternatively, some companies link EMS improvements to the environmental management program (clause 4.3.4). This approach treats identified improvements as objectives by incorporating them into the documents that chart the responsibility, means, and time frame for achieving stated targets.

The advantage offered by these approaches, which also can be employed in an integrated system, is the ability to document the initiation, implementation, and completion of system improvements in a manner that clearly depicts the current status of the system at any time.

# CHAPTER 8

## The Registration Audit

Every company that implements ISO 14001 faces the question of whether to demonstrate conformance with the standard through self-declaration or formal registration (referred to as certification outside the United States). Although ISO 14001 explicitly states that it is applicable to any organization that wishes to make a self-determination and self-declaration of conformance, it is unclear whether such declarations will be accepted by the various audiences to which they are directed.

If a state department of environmental protection determines that an ISO-14001 conforming company should be subject to less scrutiny than one without an environmental management system, or a customer uses ISO 14001 conformance as a criterion for supplier approval, it is unlikely that self-declaration will be acceptable. A company's marketplace and its interested external parties will play a significant role in determining the need for registration.

What about those companies that implement ISO 14001 because they believe it is the right thing to do, that it will improve both environmental performance and the bottom line? Even companies for which an environmental management system satisfies internal concerns rather than external imperatives can benefit from the rigor and ongoing surveillance imposed by the registration process.

One ISO 14001 registrar, NSF-ISR (Ann Arbor, Michigan) views the benefits of registration as follows:

## REASONS FOR ISO 14001 REGISTRATION

There are several reasons to register an ISO 14000 system. These reasons will vary in importance for each organization. The reasons that are most important to an organization should influence its selection of a registrar. The registration process will be, at its fundamental level, equivalent regardless of the registrar. However, the registration process design can vary, and one registrar may be more suited to an organization than another. Compatibility of a registrar's auditors with an organization and its culture can be important determining factors. Also, certain registrars' certificates may have more recognition than others in some markets because of the accreditations they hold. Accreditation differentiation will continue to diminish, however, as international multilateral agreements are signed. The International Accreditation Forum completed a multilateral agreement for ISO 9000 in January, 1998. Signatories of this agreement will accept each other's accreditations. ANSI/RAB is a signatory—consequently ANSI/RAB-accredited registrations will be accepted in the countries of other signatories. This is not yet in place for ISO 14001.

The most obvious reason for registration is that the registered organization has independent verification, substantiated by a certificate, that its management system conforms to ISO 14001. The certificate of registration provides proof of conformance to customers, upper management, the regulatory community, investors, or any other stakeholders with interest in an organization's environmental management system. Certification as a marketing tool is easily understood. It is an important reason to become registered, but experience with ISO 9000 has demonstrated that other reasons for registration are equally important. ISO 14001 registration will also provide additional benefits which ISO 9000 registration does not because the environment has a broader scope of stakeholder interest than does quality.

Organizations that have completed ISO 9000 registration and have a sustained management system often claim that a significant benefit of registration is the value that an external/independent audit brings to their system. To many, this is the most significant benefit to registration and should be considered on two levels. First, the simple fact that an audit team with no connection to the organization and

(continued)

no stake in its business plan will periodically provide an objective evaluation of the system means that an organization, at a minimum, must prepare for that audit. Therefore the system must be maintained. In the absence of this external review, systems typically degrade in performance. Once the investment has been made to establish an ISO 14001 management system, the registration and surveillance audits are analogous to an initial performance check and follow-up maintenance contract. It's a way to protect an organization's investment.

The second level of consideration is that the registrar's audit process should contribute to the continual improvement of the organization's system. The competence of the audit team and the process the registrar uses can influence the value that the audits provide. When considering a registrar, consider first its auditors. Does the registrar use auditors with environmental experience and credentials who also are experienced or have been trained in management system auditing techniques? Or does the registrar use experienced quality system auditors who have been trained to do environmental management system audits? Each of these two approaches has advocates.

It is this writer's opinion that both quality management system and environmental operations experience bring value to the registration process. But it is easier to train an experienced environmental professional about management system audit methodology than it is to teach a quality system auditor to be an environmental professional. There are two reasons for this opinion. One is that quality management system auditing is an established discipline; its methodology is teachable. The second is that environmental experience is necessary for a competent environmental management system evaluation because the standard allows for substantial management discretion in its implementation. That means that auditors must be able to make judgements relating to the conformance of the system based on environmental and management system experience. Environmental experience can't be taught. Perhaps when there is more experience with ISO 14001, the differences in the two disciplines will be managed more easily, but not at this time. If an organization values the audit process as a way to point to improvements in its system, then auditor qualifications must be carefully considered.

*(continued)*

An additional benefit of registration to ISO 14001 is the possibility of some form of regulatory benefit or flexibility. At the current time, not much is available but there will be. A growing consortium of states (currently 15) is working cooperatively with the EPA to determine how best to use ISO 14001 to benefit the environment and their mandated programs. They are also working with the European Community. This level of cooperation and coordination indicates the serious approach the regulatory community in the United States is taking to ISO 14001. Registration will be part of criteria for regulatory flexibility. These regulatory programs will be voluntary programs with incentives for participation.

Financial markets and the insurance industry are also looking at ISO 14001 as a risk management tool. There have already been reports of easier access to capital because of proactive environmental management.

These reasons to choose registration can lead to the selection of a registrar which will provide the best opportunity to achieve the desired benefit. An organization should choose its reason for registration, and then choose its registrar.

Organizations that choose not to register will spend time and money trying to convince a skeptical public, regulatory community, and financial community that their environmental management systems are acceptable. Their competitors will applaud their decision.

Gordon Bellen
Vice President, Environmental Management Systems
NSF International Strategic Registrations
Ann Arbor, Michigan 48105

Companies that integrate ISO 14001 into an existing ISO 9001/2 or QS-9000 system typically pursue ISO 14001 registration. Such companies are familiar with the registration process by virtue of having a registered quality system and integration of *anything* into the quality management system requires that the newly integrated entity is examined in conjunction with both internal quality and surveillance audits.

Registrars typically have dealt with integrated quality and environmental management systems where the quality management system is already registered by conducting an ISO 14001 registration audit and then performing integrated surveillance audits. The reregistration audit is conducted for the integrated system.

## THE ISO 14001 REGISTRATION AUDIT

The ISO 14001 registration audit process is virtually identical to quality management system registration. The audit is initiated by a formal application from the company seeking registration. Although there is no hard-and-fast rule, most registrars recommend that the system is fully functional, including employee training, internal system audit and correction of identified nonconformances, and management review, to ensure sufficient evidence of adequacy, effectiveness, and suitability.

Following receipt of the application, the registrar conducts a document review. Different registrars request different documents, but typically review

- The environmental policy
- Description of system elements (e.g., manual)
- Description of processes within the system scope
- Applicable legal requirements
- Environmental aspects and impacts
- Internal environmental management system audit reports
- Management review documents

Upon completion of the document review, a quality management system registrar would determine whether the system was ready for an on-site conformity assessment. ISO 14001 registrars, however, include an additional step before making that determination. An on-site initial assessment enables the registrar to enhance its understanding of the environmental management system and its readiness for registration.

This additional step is essential because ISO 14001 does not stipulate that all required procedures must be documented. Because a lack of documented procedures does not necessarily mean that required procedures have not been established and maintained, the registrar cannot rely on the document review to determine readiness for registration.

If the on-site initial assessment reveals objective evidence of adequate system implementation, the registrar schedules and conducts an on-site conformity assessment. The purpose of this assessment is to verify that the environmental management system conforms with all planned arrangements.

The time required for a registration audit depends primarily on the number of operations and activities that fall within the scope of the environmental management system and their environmental aspects and impacts. The size of the organization and number of employees are secondary considerations. A typical conformity assessment requires two auditors to spend three days at a facility.

Depending on the findings of the audit team, a company is approved or disapproved for registration by the registrar. Approval is granted when a company demonstrates that its system conforms to all requirements in ISO 14001 and no, or very minor, deficiencies are identified.

Conditional approval occurs when some major nonconformances are detected. Companies that are conditionally approved must submit a corrective action plan that describes how they intend to correct each identified deficiency. The registrar will conduct a follow-up audit to evaluate whether the nonconformances have been corrected. Some registrars will perform the follow-up in conjunction with scheduled surveillance audits.

Disapproval results when the system is poorly documented, poorly implemented, and poorly maintained. Disapproval is uncommon because highly deficient systems tend to be identified during the on-site initial assessment and so rarely become the subject of conformity assessment.

Once the company is registered, the registrar will continue to evaluate the system through surveillance audits. These audits, which usually occur every six months, focus on selected elements of the system. A different combination of elements is examined during each surveillance audit so that the entire system is audited over a three-year period. Surveillance audits always follow up on nonconformances detected in previous audits. Some registrars also include certain key system elements in every surveillance audit to ensure that they are properly maintained (e.g., internal EMS audits, evaluation of regulatory compliance).

## SPECIAL CONSIDERATIONS

Although ISO 14001 is not an environmental performance standard, successful implementation of the environmental management system is directly linked to improved environmental performance. In an effort to evaluate the effectiveness of the EMS, the registration auditor is likely to examine performance data as objective evidence. This can create tension between the auditor and the auditee in two areas— objectives and targets and evaluation of regulatory compliance—if these two parties interpret differently the intent of the requirements.

### Objectives and Targets

ISO 14001 requires that, among other considerations, objectives and targets reflect significant environmental impacts and the environmental policy commitment to prevention of pollution. Companies are not obligated to establish objectives and targets for every significant environmental impact; they are free to select the impacts that they wish to reduce or eliminate. It is not the registration auditor's job to second-guess either the impacts selected by a company or the targets that it attempts to achieve. However, to assure that the EMS functions effectively, the auditor may choose to examine performance measures to see whether progress in achieving a stated target is being made.

### Evaluation of Regulatory Compliance

An EMS audit is *not* a compliance audit. The registration auditor is concerned with whether a company has procedures by which it determines whether it is in compliance with all regulatory requirements and, if not, corrects identified problems. The existence of a regulatory noncompliance does not necessarily mean that the EMS fails to conform with the requirements imposed by ISO 14001. In fact, the detection of a regulatory noncompliance could be evidence that the procedure to evaluate compliance is working.

Most registrars focus on objective evidence that verifies implementation of the established procedure—for example, schedule of compliance evaluation activities, redacted compliance audit reports, records of requests for corrective action plans and their timely submission, and schedule of follow-up evaluations. Some, however, believe that actual regulatory compliance should be checked during an EMS audit to verify that the established procedure ensures compliance.

The authors recommend that companies discuss this issue during the registrar selection process. If compliance audit reports are attorney-client privileged documents that cannot be shared with a registrar, it is important to know before beginning an on-site conformity assessment whether such documents are essential to the registration process.

### Reporting Regulatory Noncompliance

Even though registrars typically do not assess regulatory compliance during an EMS audit, they may observe regulatory violations as they walk through different areas of the auditee's facility. Do such observations have to be reported? They do, but not to any regulatory agency or other external body.

Lawyers and others who have examined this issue have concluded that the registration auditor is obligated to report observed noncompliance to senior management within the audited organization. It is management's responsibility to determine the appropriate course of action, including disclosure to regulators.

One registrar explicitly states in its internal policy handbook for EMS registrations the following:

> If an auditor finds evidence of noncompliance with a law or regulation during an audit, the auditor shall report the evidence to the Company and determine whether the evidence indicates a failure of the regulatory compliance system.
>
> The Company, when informed of the evidence, shall verify the finding with the auditor, take appropriate corrective action, file all reports required by law, and report its conformance to these policies to the Registrar.
>
> The Registrar shall treat such a finding and report as confidential. In the event the auditor believes such evidence legally or ethically requires an immediate report to appropriate authorities, the auditor shall report it to the highest available level of Company management and Registrar management. The auditor shall not report it to any other parties without the authorization of the Registrar.

## THE INTEGRATED REGISTRATION AUDIT

The audit process to register a fully integrated system is virtually identical to that for QMS and EMS registration audits. However, an integrated audit imposes special considerations concerning who will conduct the audit and how it will be implemented.

Virtually every accredited ISO 14001 registrar is, first and foremost, a quality system registrar. Organizations that offered ISO 9001/2 and/or QS-9000 registration audits expanded their services to include ISO 14001 audits by hiring auditors with EMS auditing experience (not necessarily focused on ISO 14001) or employing EMS auditors on a subcontract basis. If registrars are asked to field an audit team for either a QMS or EMS audit, they can call upon qualified auditors.

Conducting an integrated audit, however, poses a challenge to registrars. Both QMS and EMS auditors are well-equipped to evaluate the generic components of both systems. After all, a document control procedure is a document control procedure, whether the documents in question are quality-related or environmental in nature. However, QMS auditors typically do not have the environmental training necessary to audit elements such as environmental aspects and impacts, identification of legal requirements, and evaluation of regulatory compliance. By the same token, EMS auditors typically do not have experience with quality issues such as contract review, design control, and product identification and traceability.

Auditors who conduct integrated system audits must be trained about and able to audit all requirements of both standards. In the near term, registrars are likely to form audit teams composed of QMS and EMS auditors. The former will audit all unique quality elements, the latter will evaluate all unique EMS elements, and both will audit the elements common to both standards. Companies seeking either an integrated system registration audit or a stand-alone ISO 14001 registration audit followed by integrated system surveillance audits should consider auditor qualifications when selecting a registrar.

Companies seeking an integrated system registration also face a challenge—ensuring that the integrated system is understood and maintained throughout the organization. Nonconformance related to either a quality matter or an environmental issue can delay the entire registration. This is of less concern to companies with registered quality systems that elect a stand-alone ISO 14001 registration followed by integrated surveillance audits. By the time such companies are ready for an integrated system reregistration audit, the feedback from the integrated surveillance audits should ensure that the whole system functions effectively.

# CHAPTER 9

## Conclusion

The benefits of integration have not been lost on the ISO Technical Management Board, which requires the Technical Committees on Quality Management and Quality Assurance (TC 176) and Environmental Management (TC 207) to improve the compatibility between ISO 9001 and ISO 14001. Compatibility between the quality and environmental management standards means that common elements of both standards can be implemented in a shared manner without unnecessary duplication. In practical terms, this means that companies will be able to implement common elements without having to accommodate seemingly different requirements. The purpose of harmonization is to revise the standards in a way that facilitates integration for those companies that choose this option.

Compatibility will be enhanced by the proposed reformatting of ISO 9001. Although the third iteration of ISO 9001 will not be finalized until 2000, the current proposed revision reorganizes the standard's 20 elements into four categories—management responsibility; resource management; management of processes; and measurement, analysis, and improvement. A table that delineates the linkages between ISO 9001 and ISO 14001 also has been proposed for inclusion in the ISO 9001 revision (see Figure 9.1). Although the format and numbering of elements is different, the intent and substance of ISO 9001 remains intact.

It is important to note that the standards themselves will not be integrated nor is there any intention to create a requirement for organizations to develop integrated systems. Keeping the standards separate will maintain the distinction between quality and environmental management, thereby allowing organizations the option to

| ISO 9001:2000 (CD 1 – July 1998) | | | ISO 14001:1996 |
|---|---|---|---|
| Quality management system requirements | 4 | 4 | Env. management system requirements |
| General | 4.1 | 4.1 | General requirements |
| Management responsibility | 5 | — | — |
| General | 5.1 | — | — |
| Customer needs and requirements | 5.2 | 4.3.2 | Legal and other requirements |
| Quality policy | 5.3 | 4.2 | Environmental policy |
| Quality objectives and planning | 5.4 | — | — |
| Quality objectives and targets | 5.4.1 | 4.3.3 | Objectives and targets |
| Quality management system | 5.5 | — | — |
| General | 5.5.1 | 4.3.4 | Environmental management program |
| Organizational structure | 5.5.2 | 4.4.1 | Structure and responsibility |
| Management representative | 5.5.3 | 4.4.1 | Structure and responsibility |
| System documentation | 5.5.4 | 4.4.4 | EMS documentation |
| Management review | 5.6 | 4.6 | Management review |
| Resource management | 6 | — | — |
| General | 6.1 | 4.3.4b | Environmental management program |
| Human resources | 6.2 | — | — |
| Designation of personnel | 6.2.1 | 4.4.1 | Structure and responsibility |
| Training and competence | 6.2.2 | 4.4.2 | Training, awareness, and competence |

Figure 9.1   Comparison of ISO 9001 (Proposed 2000 Revision) and ISO 14001 *(continued)*

| ISO 9001:2000 (CD 1 - July 1998) | | | ISO 14001:1996 |
|---|---|---|---|
| Other resources | 6.3 | — | — |
| Information | 6.3.1 | 4.4.4 | EMS documentation |
| Infrastructure | 6.3.2 | 4.3.4b | Environmental management program |
| Work environment | 6.3.3 | 4.3.4 | Environmental management program |
| Management of processes | 7 | — | — |
| Process management | 7.1 | 4.6a, b | Operational control |
| Customer | 7.2 | — | — |
| Identification of customer requirements, needs, and expectations | 7.2.1 | 4.3.2 | Legal and other requirements |
| Review of customer requirements, needs, and expectations | 7.2.2 | 4.3.2 | Legal and other requirements |
| Review of organization capability to meet defined requirements | 7.2.3 | 4.4.1 | Structure and responsibility |
| Customer communication | 7.2.4 | 4.4.3 | Communication |
| Design and development | 7.3 | 4.3.1 | Environmental aspects |
| | | 4.3.4 | Environmental management program |
| Purchasing and procurement | 7.4 | 4.4.6c | Operational control |
| Control of production and service provision operations | 7.5 | 4.4.6 | Operational control |
| Control of nonconformity | 7.6 | 4.5.2 | Nonconformance and corrective and preventive action |
| Delivery and post–delivery services | 7.7 | 4.4.6 | Operational control |

Figure 9.1  *continued*

| ISO 9001:2000 (CD 1 – July 1998) | | | ISO 14001:1996 |
|---|---|---|---|
| Measurement, analysis, and improvement | 8 | | — |
| Measurement and analysis | 8.1 | 4.5.1 | Monitoring and measurement |
| General | 8.1.1 | | — |
| Measurements of system performance | 8.1.2 | 4.5.1 | Monitoring and measurement |
| Internal audit | 8.1.2.1 | 4.5.4 | EMS audit |
| Measurements of customer satisfaction | 8.1.2.2 | 4.5.1 | Monitoring and measurement |
| Measurements of processes | 8.1.3 | 4.5.1 | Monitoring and measurement |
| Measurement of products | 8.1.4 | 4.5.1 | Monitoring and measurement |
| Control of measuring . . . test equipment | 8.1.5 | 4.5.1 | Monitoring and measurement |
| Control of quality records | 8.1.6 | 4.5.3 | Records |
| Analysis of data | 8.1.7 | 4.5.1 | Monitoring and measurement |
| Improvement | 8.2 | | — |
| Corrective action | 8.2.1 | 4.5.2 | Nonconformance and corrective and preventive action |
| Preventive action | 8.2.2 | 4.5.2 | Nonconformance and corrective and preventive action |
| Improvement processes | 8.2.3 | 4.2 / 4.6 | Environmental policy / Management review |

Figure 9.1 *concluded*

implement one rather than both. Separation also allows companies that implement both quality and environmental management systems to register only one of those systems.

It is likely that ISO efforts at compatibility will result in what many ISO-9000 registered companies already know—despite differing terminology and level of detail, the ISO 9000 series and ISO 14001 are not incompatible. Companies throughout the United States are fashioning integrated systems that leverage the strengths of the existing quality system while avoiding previously encountered pitfalls.

This book is intended to encourage critical thinking about the similarities between ISO 14001 and the ISO 9000/QS-9000 quality standards, share approaches used by various organizations in their successful implementation of an integrated system, and provide examples of documentation that have withstood the scrutiny of registrars. Understanding of the interfaces between ISO 9001 and ISO 14001, however, is not sufficient. Ultimately, the effort to integrate both systems is only as effective as the people involved.

The integration of ISO 14001 into a quality management system requires a comprehensive understanding of existing quality system processes and procedures as well as knowledge of environmental regulations and the environmental impacts associated with various operating processes. It is incumbent upon any organization that attempts to integrate its quality and environmental management systems to identify appropriate participants on its implementation team. Thus, consideration should be given to employees from both the quality assurance and environmental affairs functions, as well as employees from key operational areas such as receiving, manufacturing, shipping, purchasing, engineering, and design.

The authors hope that their insights and experience ease the transition to a fully integrated management system that infuses quality into all environmentally sensitive activities and incorporates environmental awareness into all facets of production. We have provided information to enhance understanding. It is up to you, the reader, and your colleagues to apply that understanding in your own organization. We wish you success!

# APPENDIX A

## Mega Manufacturing ISO 9002 Quality Manual

This appendix contains the ISO 9002 Quality Manual of an actual company. At the authors' request, permission to use this manual (and supporting procedures that appear in various chapters) was granted with the stipulation that we conceal the company's identity. The result, Mega Manufacturing, is an imaginary figment.

### COMPANY BACKGROUND

The Mega Manufacturing facility represented by the manuals in Appendices A and B, and the procedures presented throughout the book, is located in the southwestern United States. Employment at the 140,000-square-foot facility numbers 350. The workforce is unionized.

### A NOTE OF CAUTION

The authors' purpose in presenting this example is to illustrate how an existing quality manual can be revised to reflect an integrated system. The manual is not intended to provide a template. Rather, companies must develop their own manuals to reflect their management system and operating procedures.

| $\mathcal{MM}$ | Title: ISO 9002 Quality Manual | Page 1 of 17 |
|---|---|---|
| | | Revision: Original |
| | | Process Owner: VP, Quality Assurance |
| | | Effective Date: August 1, 1998 |
| | Steering Committee Approval | |

(0.0) Introduction

Mega Manufacturing, 1234 Main Street, Big City, New Mexico 54321

Phone: 505-555-1111; Fax: 505-555-2222

Mega Manufacturing has been in uninterrupted existence since 1946 and has concentrated solely on the manufacture and repair of diesel truck engines since 1975. Since its inception, the Company has enjoyed an excellent reputation in the industry.

Mega Manufacturing operates under a documented quality program that complies with ISO 9002.

Mega Manufacturing is composed of two divisions: Service Division and Engine Manufacture Division. This Quality System Manual applies to the Service Division only. When the Engine Service Division performs services for the Engine Manufacture Division, it is a customer-supplier relationship.

(0.1) Approvals

Mega Manufacturing employees, at all levels, are committed to becoming the premier diesel engine service center in the world, and this commitment is evidenced in the Mega Manufacturing Mission Statement shown in Appendix A of this manual. Each employee has been indoctrinated with the Company's mission statements.

_____          _____
President                       VP, Quality Assurance

_____          _____
VP, Operations                  VP, Engineering

_____              _____

VP, Finance/Administration           VP & General Manager

_____              _____

VP, Marketing & Sales                VP & General Counsel


(1.0) Scope and Field of Application

(1.1) Scope

This manual describes a quality system that demonstrates Mega Manufacturing's capability to control their processes and to ensure that an acceptable product is supplied to our customers. The system ensures detection of all nonconformances during production and installation and incorporates a means to prevent their recurrence.

(1.2) Field of Application

The policies described in this manual apply to all products and services provided by Mega Manufacturing, Service Division, located at 1234 Main Street, Big City, New Mexico 54321.

(2.0) References

This manual was developed to meet the requirements of ISO 9002.

(3.0) Definitions/Acronyms

For purposes of this manual the definitions given in ISO 8402 apply. In this manual the term *product* is also used to denote *service* as appropriate. In some instances in this manual the term *nonconformance* refers to engines, modules, or parts that have incorporated a defect resulting from normal in-service usage and/or wear. This is actually incoming condition assessment damage and is not an actual nonconformance.

> Incoming condition—Condition of an engine, module, or part as received from the customer. Incoming condition may include deviations from the specification/manual requirement.

> Nonconformance—A deviation from a standard practice/ technical requirement that is generated or continued to exist beyond the point in the repair cycle where the deviation should have been reworked, repaired, or otherwise removed.

OEM—Original equipment manufacturer

PCM—Process control manual

SPM—Shop procedures manual

(4.0) Quality System Requirements

(4.1) Management Responsibility

This manual defines and documents the Mega Manufacturing quality objectives and the Company's commitment to quality.

(4.1.1) Quality Policy

The Quality Policy at Mega Manufacturing is to provide our customers with the highest quality engine maintenance services, meet our commitments with respect to specifications, turn time and cost, and to accomplish this in a manner to support Mega Manufacturing's Mission as defined in Appendix A of this manual. Mega Manufacturing will utilize all available resources to continually improve its capabilities. The executive staff is committed to this policy throughout, and the approval of such is supported by their signatures in this manual.

Mega Manufacturing commits itself to meet its customers' expectations with regards to *quality, turn time,* and *cost.* It challenges its workforce to live up to this commitment while providing incentives, a respectable work environment, and an excellent compensation package.

Mega Manufacturing developed its mission/vision statement, and each production cell or working group has complemented the Company's statement with individual mission statements developed by employees within those areas. These mission statements are displayed throughout the facility.

(4.1.2) Organization

Mega Manufacturing Management Organization:

President

VP, Marketing & Sales

VP & General Manager, Latin America Sales/Parts

VP, Operations

VP, Quality Assurance

VP, Engineering

VP, Finance/Administration

VP & General Counsel

(4.1.2.1) Responsibility and Authority

Mega Manufacturing Board of Directors has charged the President of Mega Manufacturing with the responsibility and freedom of management and administrative control of the overall operation. This includes the basic resources of capital, facilities, equipment, and people, and to exercise the primary managing responsibilities of planning an organization with a quality-oriented culture.

Mega Manufacturing executive management has charged the Vice President of Quality Assurance and the quality organization with the responsibility, authority, and freedom to initiate and document action to prevent the occurrence of any nonconformances relating to the product, process, and quality system and to initiate, recommend, or provide corrective actions and to verify the implementation of these corrective actions. It further grants it the authority to stop processing, delivery, or installation of nonconforming product until the deficiency has been corrected.

Mega Manufacturing executive management has charged the Vice President of Engineering and the engineering organization with the responsibility, authority, and freedom to develop, implement, and document quality plans to prevent the occurrence of nonconformances.

Mega Manufacturing executive management has charged the Vice President of Operations and the operations organization with the responsibility, authority, and freedom to assure procedural compliance with all service demands, and to provide ongoing improvements to the engine repair process cycle that maximizes reliability, optimizes quality and turn-time, and minimizes costs.

Mega Manufacturing executive management has charged the Vice President of Finance/Administration and the finance/administration organization with the responsibility, authority, and freedom to assure procedural compliance with all service demands and to provide ongoing material requirements and improvements to the engine repair process cycle that maximizes reliability, optimizes quality and turn-time, and minimizes costs.

Mega Manufacturing executive management has charged the Vice President of Marketing & Sales, the Vice President & General Manager, and the marketing and sales organization with the responsibility, authority, and freedom to assure the customer requirements are adequately defined and documented. Mega Manufacturing has the capability to perform before any contract is accepted with respect to quality, turn-time, and cost.

Mega Manufacturing executive management has charged the Vice President General Counsel with the responsibility, authority, and freedom to assure compliance with all legal requirements from the regulatory agencies.

(4.1.2.2) Resources

The President of Mega Manufacturing has given each Vice President the authority to identify and provide the required resources, including trained personnel, for all the performance activities within their organizations including internal quality audits. Activities shall include inspection, test, and monitoring of the production and installation or processes and/or products.

(4.1.2.3) Management Representative

Mega Manufacturing executive management has appointed the Vice President of Quality Assurance as the Management Representative and has given him/her the authority to establish, implement, and maintain a quality system in accordance with ISO 9002.

(4.1.3) Management Review

Mega Manufacturing management with executive responsibility reviews Mega Manufacturing's quality system at least quarterly to ensure its continued stability and effectiveness in satisfying the requirements of ISO 9002 as well as the Mega Manufacturing quality policy and objectives. Actions from these reviews are recorded on a Corrective Action Plan and assigned to a Vice President to review and take appropriate action at the next meeting. For additional details, see Quality System Procedure #40.10.

(4.2) Quality System

(4.2.1) General

Mega Manufacturing has developed, implemented, and is maintaining a quality system as a means of ensuring that the product conforms to the specified requirements. In addition to this manual, the documented quality system is contained in the following Mega Manufacturing manuals.

Shop Procedures Manual (SPM)—The SPM is used to provide the details by which Mega Manufacturing controls the overhaul/repair of engines. As detail work instructions are developed, this manual will be phased out. If a conflict exists between this manual and the ISO System Level Procedures and/or ISO detail work instructions, the ISO procedures/instructions will be followed.

Process Control Manual (PCM)—The PCM is used to provide processes which consolidate approved data from many sources into one document.

System Level Procedures (SLP)—SLPs are used to describe how the system is implemented, operating controls for the quality processes, and system and interdepartmental flows and control.

Detail Work Instructions (DWI)—DWIs are used to give specific instructions on how to perform specific duties, prepare forms, and handle intradepartmental activities.

Engineering Order—An engineering order is used to release for accomplishment, authorized repairs, installations, removals, or modifications to an engine and/or component.

Shop Information Bulletin (SIB)—The SIB provides the shop with advanced and/or general information which may not be available in the manufacturing manual, such as problems encountered by other shops, in-service problems, etc.

(4.2.2) Quality System Procedures

Mega Manufacturing has developed, documented, implemented, and is maintaining quality procedures consistent with the requirements of ISO 9002.

Procedure 40.20 was issued to provide Mega Manufacturing with a uniform preparation and approval system for Mega Manufacturing quality system documents and to ensure that obsolete documents are archived.

The numbering system being used for the quality manual, procedures, and instructions follows the ISO 9002 numbering system (for example, 4.2 in ISO 9002 appears as 4.2 in the quality manual). System level procedures are *times 10* (for example, 4.2 in ISO 9002 or the quality manual appears as 40.20 in the procedures). Detail work instructions are *times 100* (for example, 4.2 in ISO 9002 or the quality manual and/or 40.20 in the procedures appears as 400.200 in the work instructions). For additional details, see Quality System Procedure #40.20.

(4.2.3) Quality Planning

The initial quality and test planning is performed at the earliest practical phase of the contract and/or purchase order. The activities are coordinated so that specific quality and test functions can be effectively directed and their accomplishments and effectiveness measured. For additional details, see Quality System Procedure #40.22.

(4.3) Contract Review

(4.3.1) General

Mega Manufacturing procedures ensure that all affected departments provide needed information to Marketing in order to ensure that Mega Manufacturing has the capability, both technically and financially, of providing for customer requirements as specified in the contract proposal before it is presented to a customer.

(4.3.2) Review

The Vice President of Marketing and Sales and the Vice President & General Manager have developed and implemented procedures to review contracts to assure Mega Manufacturing has the capability to meet the contractual requirements and that the requirements are adequately defined and documented. Procedures are in place to permit amendment to contracts, as required, and include all functions of the organization involved with the amendment. This is accomplished by a Proposal Team put together by the Proposal Manager for each contract.

The team assigned is also responsible for assuring the requirements of the issued contract are the same as the tender. The team maintains records of contract reviews. For additional details, see Quality System Procedures #40.30 and #40.31.

(4.4) Design Control

Mega Manufacturing is not a designer of diesel engines.

(4.5) Document and Data Control

(4.5.1) General

The Vice President of Engineering has implemented and documented a system that assures all documents and data are reviewed and approved prior to being issued and are controlled to the requirements of ISO 9002. Copies of the appropriate controlled documents (hard copy or computer generated) are available at all locations where they are required. The system includes procedures to remove obsolete documents and data.

(4.5.2) Document and Data Approval and Issue

Procedures exist for the control of aperture cards, data, microfilm tapes, microfiche, manuals, forms, routers, and imaged documents to assure that the only documents used are both approved and the correct revision.

(4.5.3) Document and Data Changes

Revisions to procedures are approved by the same functions/organizations that performed the original approval unless specifically designated otherwise. The designated functions should have access to pertinent data and information upon which to base their review. This procedure requires that the nature of all changes to Mega Manufacturing documents (excludes documents issued by OEMs, specifications, and regulatory agencies) are identified. A revision system (master list) is in place to assure documents are reissued after each change and that all work is performed in accordance with the latest revision to the documents. For additional details, see Quality System Procedures #40.50, #40.51, #40.52, #40.53, and #40.54.

(4.6) Purchasing

(4.6.1) General

Mega Manufacturing ensures that all purchased products and services conform to specified requirements.

(4.6.2) Evaluation of Subcontractors

Mega Manufacturing selects subcontractors on the basis of their ability to meet subcontract requirements, including quality requirements. Records are maintained on all acceptable subcontractors. The control exercised is dependent upon the type of product and, where appropriate, on records of the subcontractors' previously demonstrated capability and performance. Audits are conducted to assure the effectiveness of the Mega Manufacturing supplier control system. For additional details, see Quality System Procedure #40.61.

(4.6.3) Purchasing Data

Mega Manufacturing reviews and approves purchasing documents to assure requirements clearly describe the product or service ordered. Purchased material for engine, module, or part production is purchased from Mega Manufacturing approved sources. The purchase order requires the vendors to comply with all rework and processes as stated in the OEM overhaul or repair manual. Purchasing documents shall be reviewed for adequacy of specified requirements prior to release.

(4.6.4) Verification of Purchased Product

(4.6.4.1) Supplier Verification at Subcontractor's Premises

If required, purchase documents will specify that on-site inspections will be performed by personnel from Mega Manufacturing before release of the product from the supplier.

(4.6.4.2) Customer Verification of Subcontracted Product

Mega Manufacturing, Mega Manufacturing's representative, and Mega Manufacturing's customer or their representative have the right to verify, at the source or upon receipt, that purchased product conforms to the specification. Verification by the customer does not absolve Mega Manufacturing of its responsibility to provide acceptable products nor does it preclude the customer's right to reject the product. It also does not preclude the customer's subsequent right to rejection. For additional details, see Quality System Procedure #40.60.

(4.7) Control of Customer-Supplied Product

Mega Manufacturing has implemented and maintains procedures for verification, storage, and maintenance of customer-supplied product provided for incorporation into their engines, modules, or parts. Product that is lost, damaged, or otherwise unsuitable for use shall be recorded and reported to the customer. This reporting does not absolve Mega Manufacturing of the responsibility to provide acceptable engines, modules, or parts. For additional details, see Quality System Procedure #40.70.

(4.8) Product Identification and Traceability

Where, and to the extent that, traceability is a specified requirement, Mega Manufacturing has implemented and maintains procedures for identifying traceability of the required product and the quality status during all stages of production and delivery. Each engine, module, or part is assigned and recorded a unique work order number. For additional details, see Quality System Procedure #40.80.

(4.9) Process Control

Mega Manufacturing has implemented and maintains production plans that directly affect quality and ensures that these processes are carried out under controlled conditions. These plans include, but are not limited to, documented work instructions defining the manner of production, tooling to be used, environment, compliance with referenced standards/codes, and quality plans. The system includes monitoring and control of suitable processes and product characteristics during production. The system also incorporates approval of processes, process operators, and equipment as required. The quality plan includes written criteria for workmanship standards. The Mega Manufacturing Training Manager maintains records to assure all special process operators are qualified or certified as required by specifications. The Production Manager of the Support Shops maintains records of special process equipment to ensure its continuing process capability. For additional details, see Quality System Procedures #40.90, #40.91, #40.92, #40.93, #40.94, #40.95, and #40.96.

(4.10) Inspection and Testing

(4.10.1) General

Mega Manufacturing has established and maintains inspection and testing activities through documented procedures and work instructions to verify compliance with required specifications and to maintain records that provide evidence that the product has been inspected and tested.

(4.10.2) Receiving Inspection and Testing

(4.10.2.1) Mega Manufacturing's quality plan requires incoming engine, module, or parts be inspected or otherwise verified as conforming to the specified requirements prior to use of processing unless a prerelease has been issued and approved by the Vice President of Quality Assurance, Vice President of Operations, and the applicable Shop Manager. Verification shall be in accordance with the established quality plan and/or other documented procedures.

(4.10.2.2) The Receiving Inspector determines if he/she accepts the material or sends the material to detail inspection for a more in-depth inspection.

(4.10.2.3) In the event incoming engine, module, or part is released for urgent production purposes, it shall be positively identified and recorded via the *Prerelease* SPM 15-80 in order to permit immediate recall and replacement in the event a nonconformance is verified.

(4.10.3) In-Process Inspection and Testing

Mega Manufacturing's quality plan requires that engines, modules, and parts shall not be released until all required inspections have been completed unless a prerelease has been issued and approved by the Vice President of Quality Assurance, Vice President of Operations, and the applicable Shop Manager. The required inspections insure that engines, modules, and parts conform to specified requirements.

(4.10.4) Final Inspection and Testing

The Mega Manufacturing quality plan and documented procedures assure complete evidence of conformance of the finished engines, modules, and parts to the specified requirements, which assures all required receiving, in-process, and final inspections and tests have been completed. No engines, modules, or parts shall be delivered until the complete quality plan has been accomplished and evidence of conformance to the specified requirements is documented, available, and the release is authorized.

(4.10.5) Inspection and Test Records

Mega Manufacturing maintains records which give evidence that the product has passed inspection and/or test with defined acceptance criteria. The Training Manager is responsible for maintaining the Authorized Inspection List. For additional details, see Quality System Procedure #40.100.

(4.11) Control of Inspection, Measuring, and Test Equipment

(4.11.1) General

Mega Manufacturing maintains a calibration laboratory as a function of quality assurance. The calibration laboratory developed, implemented, and maintains a plan which assures all measurement and test equipment, including test software, is controlled by the plan for both company-owned and personal tools. The quality plan identifies the measurements to be made and where they are to be made in the process. The plan requires records be generated and maintained that identify all calibrations, adjustments, and repairs made on measurement and test equipment. Equipment shall be used in a manner which ensures that measurement uncertainty is known and is consistent with the required measurement capability. The procedure provides provisions for the customer to confirm measuring and/or test results related to engines, modules, and parts they have contracted to have repaired.

(4.11.2) Control Procedure

1. All required measurements are specified by Engineering via the quality plan for the engine, module, and/or part. The inspector or mechanic will select the correct measuring and test equipment from the published document "Accuracy Use Limits for Standard Measuring Instruments."
2. The plan requires records be generated and maintained that identify all calibrations, adjustments, and repairs made on measurement and test equipment were performed

in accordance with the National Institute of Standards and Technology and/or documented Mega Manufacturing standards.

3. Mega Manufacturing documented calibration procedures define the methods, equipment, frequency, acceptance criteria, and action to be taken.

4. The individual who performed the calibration will be identified on the record, and the date the next calibration is due will be identified on the measuring equipment.

5. The plan requires the Manager of Quality Control be notified when inspection, measuring, and test equipment is found to be out of calibration.

6. The procedure specifies the environmental conditions suitable to perform calibration and specifies handling, preservation, and storage instruction of inspection and test equipment. Measuring and test equipment will be stored in suitable containers to protect it from adverse conditions that could affect the accuracy of the equipment.

7. If measuring and test equipment is tampered with, dropped, or damaged, it is immediately returned to the Calibration Laboratory for the appropriate action. For additional details, see Quality System Procedure #40.110.

(4.12) Inspection and Test Status

Mega Manufacturing's quality plan requires the inspection and test status of engines, modules, and parts be identified by suitable means, which will indicate the conformance or nonconformance of the engines, modules, and parts with regard to inspections and tests performed. The identification of inspection and test status shall be maintained as defined in the quality plan (see SLP 40.22) throughout production of the engines, modules, and parts to ensure that only engines, modules, and parts that have passed necessary inspections and test are shipped to the customer. Records are maintained that identify those individuals authorized to release conforming engines, modules, and parts. For additional details, see Quality System Procedure #40.120.

(4.13) Control of Nonconforming Product

(4.13.1) General

Mega Manufacturing has implemented and maintains a procedure to ensure engines, modules, and parts that do not conform to the specified requirements are identified, documented, evaluated, dispositioned, and segregated to prevent them from unintended use. Notification of the nonconformance will be given to all responsible affected parties, and records will identify the inspection authority responsible for the release of nonconforming engines, modules, and parts.

(4.13.2) Review and Disposition of Nonconforming Product

Mega Manufacturing procedures specify who has the authority to disposition nonconforming engines, modules, and parts. This is accomplished in accordance with the appropriate procedures, and when required, the customer is notified of any nonconformance. Nonconforming engines, modules, and parts may be reworked to meet the specified requirements, accepted without repair, or scrapped in accordance with the customer's requirement. Engines, modules, and parts that are repaired and/or reworked shall be reinspected in accordance with the quality plan and/or documented procedures. For additional details, see Quality System Procedure #40.130.

(4.14) Corrective and Preventive Action

(4.14.1) General

Mega Manufacturing has implemented and maintains a procedure to assure that adequate investigation and corrective and preventive action is taken to eliminate the cause of nonconformances. As part of the investigation, controls are in place to assure the effectiveness of the corrective and preventive action.

(4.14.2) Corrective Action

Mega Manufacturing procedures apply to all nonconformances identified from internal/external quality audits, customer complaints, employee-discovered discrepancies, and chargeable test cell rejects. The procedures require analyzing processes, work operations, quality records, and customer complaints to detect and eliminate causes of nonconformances. Corrective actions taken to eliminate the nonconformance are documented in the Nonconformance Database Log.

## (4.14.3) Preventive Action

Mega Manufacturing procedures apply to all nonconformances identified from internal/external quality audits, customer complaints, employee-discovered discrepancies, and chargeable test cell rejects. The procedures require analyzing processes, work operations, quality records, and customer complaints to detect and eliminate causes of nonconformances. Actions are taken to insure that a preventive action program is established to eliminate the potential causes of nonconformance documented in the Nonconformance Database Log. The Vice President of Quality Assurance will review all open corrective/preventive actions with the Executive Quality Committee on at least a quarterly basis. During this review, if any follow-up is required it will be assigned to the Mega Manufacturing ISO Audit Team. For additional details, see Quality System Procedure #40.140.

## (4.15) Handling, Storage, Packaging, Preservation, and Delivery

## (4.15.1) General

Mega Manufacturing has implemented and maintains procedures for the handling, storage, packaging, and delivery of engines, modules, and parts.

## (4.15.2) Handling

Mega Manufacturing procedures require suitable trays, racks, stands, protective coverings, and other measures be provided to ensure maximum protection of all engines, modules, and parts, including protection from damage or deterioration.

## (4.15.3) Storage

Mega Manufacturing provides secure storage areas that prevent damage or deterioration of engines, modules, and parts pending their use or delivery. The Shipping and Receiving area maintains records of all incoming and outgoing engines, modules, and parts.

Periodic audits of the storage areas are performed to ensure that all engines, modules, and parts are protected from damage and/or deterioration.

(4.15.4) Packaging

Mega Manufacturing procedures control packing and marking processes, including materials used, to ensure conformance to the requirements from receiving to shipping.

(4.15.5) Preservation

Mega Manufacturing procedures control shelf life, preservation, and segregation of engines, modules, and parts to ensure conformance to the requirements from receiving to shipping.

(4.15.6) Delivery

Mega Manufacturing procedures provide for the protection of the engines, modules, and parts after final inspection and test and prior to delivery. If contractually specified, protection shall be expanded to point of delivery to customer. For additional details, see Quality System Procedures #40.151 and #40.152.

(4.16) Control of Quality Records

Mega Manufacturing has implemented and maintains a procedure that specifies the method of collecting, indexing, accessing, filing, storing, maintaining, and dispositioning all quality records. Mega Manufacturing shop processing and subcontractors' records are audited to assure they are legible and complete before being stored in a suitable environment to minimize deterioration or damage. The records shall be stored and maintained in such a way that they can be readily retrieved. Where agreed contractually, quality records shall be made available for evaluation by the customer or his representative. Records' retention times are established by contract with the customer. For additional details, see Quality System Procedure #40.160.

(4.17) Internal Quality Audits

Mega Manufacturing has implemented and maintains a system of internal quality audits in accordance with the established procedures to verify the effectiveness of the quality system. The Vice President of Quality Assurance is responsible for establishing an audit schedule according to the importance of the activity being audited, assigning the auditors, and ensuring that follow-up actions are appropriate. All audits are documented and brought to the attention of the management personnel responsible for the area audited. The management personnel are responsible for taking timely corrective action on the deficiencies found by the audit. The Vice President of Quality Assurance will review all open audits with the Quality Executive Committee on at least a quarterly basis. For additional details, see Quality System Procedures #40.170 and #40.171.

(4.18) Training

Mega Manufacturing has implemented and maintains procedures that identify the training needs of all personnel performing activities affecting quality. Appropriate training is provided in a timely manner. Records are maintained on these employees to assure they are qualified to perform the required work. Those employees that are required by regulation to be periodically certified in their job performance are monitored, and records are maintained to show they have satisfied all certification requirements. For additional details, see Quality System Procedure #40.180.

(4.19) Servicing

Mega Manufacturing has implemented and maintains a procedure that provides an orderly response to a customer request for engine field service and assures a documented, quality repair is performed in a minimum time frame. For additional details, see Quality System Procedure #40.190.

(4.20) Statistical Techniques

(4.20.1) Identification of Need

Mega Manufacturing has implemented and maintains a procedure to ensure adequate statistical techniques are applied to verify the acceptability of processes and deliverable product.

(4.20.2) Procedures

Mega Manufacturing's procedure controls the implementation of all statistical techniques determined to be required to control the quality of engines, modules, parts, and/or process capability. For additional details, see Quality System Procedure #40.200.

# APPENDIX A

## Mega Manufacturing Mission Statement

Mega Manufacturing will strive to become the premier truck diesel engine service center worldwide. We will accomplish this by providing

- Our *customers* with the highest quality engine maintenance services and meeting our commitments with respect to specifications, turn time, and cost
- Our *employees* with challenging work assignments, a respectable work environment, and an excellent compensation package
- Our *shareholders* with a superior return on investment

# APPENDIX B

## Mega Manufacturing Integrated System Manual

The ISO 9002 Quality Manual presented in Appendix A provides the basis for an integrated system manual that reflects both ISO 9002 and ISO 14001. The integrated manual reflects the organizational structure depicted in Figure 4.1.

This example is specific to an actual company (described in Appendix A) and illustrates the application of its own quality procedures and practices to the requirements of ISO 14001. It is not intended as a template. Rather, its purpose is to demonstrate how the QMS and EMS can be documented in a single manual.

Only those sections of the quality manual that have been revised are presented here. Revisions are presented in **_bold italics_** for clarity. Because the manual is not reproduced in its entirety, page numbers and other identifying information are not provided at the bottom of every page.

| _MM_ Title: ISO 9002/14001 System | Page 1 of 17 |
|---|---|
| Manual | |
| | Revision: _1_ |
| | Process Owner: VP, Quality Assurance |
| | Effective Date: _September 1,_ 1998 |
| Steering Committee Approval | |

(0.0) Introduction

Mega Manufacturing, 1234 Main Street, Big City, New Mexico 54321
Phone: 505-555-1111; Fax: 505-555-2222

Mega Manufacturing has been in uninterrupted existence since 1946 and has concentrated solely on the manufacture and repair of diesel truck engines since 1975. Since its inception, the Company has enjoyed an excellent reputation in the industry.

Mega Manufacturing operates under a documented _integrated_ quality-_environmental management_ program that complies with ISO 9002 _and ISO 14001._

Mega Manufacturing is composed of two divisions: Service Division and Engine Manufacture Division. This _System Manual_ applies to the Service Division only. When the Engine Service Division performs services for the Engine Manufacture Division, it is a customer-supplier relationship.

(0.1) Approvals

Mega Manufacturing employees, at all levels, are committed to becoming the premier diesel engine service center in the world, and this commitment is evidenced in the Mega Manufacturing Mission Statement shown in Appendix A of this manual. Each employee has been indoctrinated with the Company's mission statements.

_____         _____
President                                        VP, Quality Assurance

_____         _____
VP, Operations                              VP, Engineering

| | |
|---|---|
| _____ | _____ |
| VP, Finance/Administration | VP & General Manager |

| | |
|---|---|
| _____ | _____ |
| VP, Marketing & Sales | VP & General Counsel |

(1.0) Scope and Field of Application

(1.1) Scope

This manual describes *an integrated* quality-*environmental management* system that demonstrates Mega Manufacturing's capability to control their processes *and significant environmental impacts* and to ensure that an acceptable product is supplied to our customers. The system ensures detection of all nonconformances during production and installation and incorporates a means to prevent their recurrence.

(1.1) Field of Application

The policies described in this manual apply to all products and services provided by Mega Manufacturing, Service Division, located at 1234 Main Street, Big City, New Mexico 54321.

(2.0) References

This manual was developed to meet the requirements of ISO 9002 *and ISO 14001.*

(3.0) Definitions/Acronyms

For purposes of this manual the definitions given in ISO 8402 *and ISO 14050* apply. In this manual the term *product* is also used to denote *service* as appropriate. In some instances in this manual the term *nonconformance* refers to engines, modules, or parts that have incorporated a defect resulting from normal in-service usage and/or wear. This is actually incoming condition assessment damage and is not an actual nonconformance.

Incoming condition—Condition of an engine, module, or part as received from the customer. Incoming condition may include deviations from the specification/manual requirement.

Nonconformance—A deviation from a standard practice/ technical requirement that is generated or continued to exist beyond the point in the repair cycle where the deviation should have been reworked, repaired, or otherwise removed

OEM—Original equipment manufacturer

PCM—Process control manual

SPM—Shop procedures manual

(4.0) *Integrated* Quality-*Environmental Management* System Requirements

(4.1) Management Responsibility

This manual defines and documents the Mega Manufacturing quality *and environmental* objectives and the Company's commitment to quality *and prevention of pollution.*

(4.1.1) Quality *and Environmental Policies*

The Quality Policy at Mega Manufacturing is to provide our customers with the highest quality engine maintenance services, meet our commitments with respect to specifications, turn time and cost, and to accomplish this in a manner to support Mega Manufacturing's Mission as defined in Appendix A of this manual. Mega Manufacturing will utilize all available resources to continually improve its capabilities. The executive staff is committed to this policy throughout, and the approval of such is supported by their signatures in this manual.

Mega Manufacturing commits itself to meet its customers' expectations with regards to *quality, turn time,* and *cost.* It challenges its workforce to live up to this commitment while providing incentives, a respectable work environment, and an excellent compensation package.

*The Environmental Policy at Mega Manufacturing is to operate in compliance with all applicable local, state, and federal environmental regulations, consider prevention of pollution in all operations and activities, and continually improve our operations and activities to protect our environment.*

Mega Manufacturing developed its mission/vision statement, and each production cell or working group has complemented the Company's statement with individual mission statements developed by employees within those areas. These mission statements are displayed throughout the facility.

(4.1.2) Organization

Mega Manufacturing Management Organization:

President

VP, Marketing & Sales

VP & General Manager, Latin America Sales/Parts

VP, Operations

VP, Quality Assurance

VP, Engineering

VP, Finance/Administration

VP & General Counsel

(4.1.2.1) Responsibility and Authority

Mega Manufacturing Board of Directors has charged the President of Mega Manufacturing with the responsibility and freedom of management and administrative control of the overall operation. This includes the basic resources of capital, facilities, equipment, and people, and to exercise the primary managing responsibilities of planning an organization with a quality-oriented culture.

Mega Manufacturing executive management has charged the Vice President of Quality Assurance and the quality organization with the responsibility, authority, and freedom to initiate and document action to prevent the occurrence of any nonconformances relating to the product, process, *and integrated* quality-*environmental management* system and to initiate, recommend, or provide corrective actions and to verify the implementation of these corrective actions. It further grants it the authority to stop processing, delivery, or installation of nonconforming product until the deficiency has been corrected.

Mega Manufacturing executive management has charged the Vice President of Engineering and the engineering organization with the responsibility, authority, and freedom to develop, implement, and document quality *and environmental management* plans to prevent the occurrence of nonconformances, *and to assure that all plans issued comply with all regulatory agencies' requirements.*

Mega Manufacturing executive management has charged the Vice President of Operations and the operations organization with the responsibility, authority, and freedom to assure procedural compliance with all service demands *and legal requirements from the regulatory agencies, to minimize environmental impacts,* and to provide ongoing improvements to the engine repair process cycle that maximizes reliability, optimizes quality and turn-time, and minimizes costs.

Mega Manufacturing executive management has charged the Vice President of Finance/Administration and the finance/administration organization with the responsibility, authority, and freedom to assure procedural compliance with all service demands and to provide ongoing material requirements and improvements to the engine repair process cycle that maximizes reliability, optimizes quality and turn-time, and minimizes costs.

Mega Manufacturing executive management has charged the Vice President of Marketing & Sales, the Vice President & General Manager, and the marketing and sales organization with the responsibility, authority, and freedom to assure the customer requirements are adequately defined and documented. Mega Manufacturing has the capability to perform before any contract is accepted with respect to quality, turn-time, and cost.

Mega Manufacturing executive management has charged the Vice President General Counsel with the responsibility, authority, and freedom to assure compliance with all legal requirements from the regulatory agencies.

(4.1.2.2) Resources
The President of Mega Manufacturing has given each Vice President the authority to identify and provide the required resources, including trained personnel, for all the performance activities within their organizations including internal *system* audits. Activities shall include inspection, test, and monitoring of the production and installation or processes and/or products.

(4.1.2.3) Management Representative
Mega Manufacturing executive management has appointed the Vice President of Quality Assurance as the Management Representative and has given him/her the authority to establish, implement, and

maintain *an integrated* quality-*environmental management* system in accordance with ISO 9002 *and ISO 14001.*

(4.1.3) Management Review

Mega Manufacturing management with executive responsibility reviews Mega Manufacturing's *integrated* system at least quarterly to ensure its continued stability and effectiveness in satisfying the requirements of ISO 9002 *and ISO 14001* as well as the Mega Manufacturing quality *and environmental policies* and objectives. Actions from these reviews are recorded on a Corrective Action Plan and assigned to a Vice President to review and take appropriate action at the next meeting. For additional details, see *System* Procedure #40.10.

(4.2) Quality-*Environmental Management* System

(4.2.1) General

Mega Manufacturing has developed, implemented, and is maintaining *an integrated* quality-*environmental management* system as a means of ensuring that the product conforms to the specified requirements *and pollution is minimized in all operations and activities.* In addition to this manual, the documented *system* is contained in the following Mega Manufacturing manuals.

Shop Procedures Manual (SPM)—The SPM is used to provide the details by which Mega Manufacturing controls the overhaul/repair of engines. As detail work instructions are developed, this manual will be phased out. If a conflict exists between this manual and the ISO System Level Procedures and/or ISO detail work instructions, the ISO procedures/instructions will be followed.

Process Control Manual (PCM)—The PCM is used to provide processes which consolidate approved data from many sources into one document.

System Level Procedures (SLP)—SLPs are used to describe how the system is implemented, operating controls for the quality *and environmental management* processes, and system and interdepartmental flows and control.

Detail Work Instructions (DWI)—DWIs are used to give specific instructions on how to perform specific duties, prepare forms, and handle intradepartmental activities.

Engineering Order—An engineering order is used to release for accomplishment, authorized repairs, installations, removals, or modifications to an engine and/or component.

Shop Information Bulletin (SIB)—The SIB provides the shop with advanced and/or general information which may not be available in the manufacturing manual, such as problems encountered by other shops, in-service problems, etc.

(4.2.2) System *Level* Procedures

Mega Manufacturing has developed, documented, implemented, and is maintaining *procedures* consistent with the requirements of ISO 9002 *and ISO 14001.*

Procedure 40.20 was issued to provide Mega Manufacturing with a uniform preparation and approval system for Mega Manufacturing quality-*environmental management* system documents and to ensure that obsolete documents are archived.

The numbering system being used for the *system* manual, procedures, and instructions follows the ISO 9002 numbering system (for example, 4.2 in ISO 9002 appears as 4.2 in the *system* manual). *Elements from ISO 14001 are integrated into the system manual according to the index in Appendix B to this manual.* System level procedures are *times 10* (for example, 4.2 in ISO 9002 or the *system* manual appears as 40.20 in the procedures). Detail work instructions are *times 100* (for example, 4.2 in ISO 9002 or the *system* manual and/or 40.20 in the procedures appears as 400.200 in the work instructions. For additional details, see *System* Procedure #40.20.

(4.2.3) *Planning*

The initial quality and test planning is performed at the earliest practical phase of the contract and/or purchase order. The activities are coordinated so that specific quality and test functions can be effectively directed and their accomplishments and effectiveness measured. For additional details, see *System* Procedure #40.22.

*Environmental planning encompasses four related activities. Environmental aspects and impacts are identified and evaluated for every operation and activity. Environmental legal requirements pertaining to all operations and activities also are identified. Mega Manufacturing determines objectives and targets to effectively address identified significant environmental impacts and regulatory requirements and provides adequate resources to achieve objectives and targets. For additional details, see System Procedures #40.23 and #40.24.*

Clauses 4.3 and 4.4 are left out because no revision regarding ISO 14001 is required.

(4.5) Document and Data Control

(4.5.1) General

The Vice President of Engineering has implemented and documented a system that assures all documents and data are reviewed and approved prior to being issued and are controlled to the requirements of ISO 9002 *and ISO 14001.* Copies of the appropriate controlled documents (hard copy or computer generated) are available at all locations where they are required. The system includes procedures to remove obsolete documents and data.

(4.5.2) Document and Data Approval and Issue

Procedures exist for the control of aperture cards, data, microfilm tapes, microfiche, manuals, forms, routers, and imaged documents to assure that the only documents used are both approved and the correct revision.

(4.5.3) Document and Data Changes

Revisions to procedures are approved by the same functions/organizations that performed the original approval unless specifically designated otherwise. The designated functions should have access to pertinent data and information upon which to base their review. This procedure requires that the nature of all changes to Mega Manufacturing documents (excludes documents issued by OEMs, specifications, and regulatory agencies) are identified. A revision system (master list) is in place to assure documents are reissued after each change and that all work is performed in accordance with the latest revision to the documents. For additional details, see *System* Procedures #40.50, #40.51, #40.52, #40.53, and #40.54.

(4.6) Purchasing

(4.6.1) General

Mega Manufacturing ensures that all purchased products and services conform to specified requirements.

(4.6.2) Evaluation of Subcontractors

Mega Manufacturing selects subcontractors on the basis of their ability to meet subcontract requirements, including quality *and prevention of pollution* requirements. Records are maintained on all acceptable subcontractors. The control exercised is dependent upon the type of product and, where appropriate, on records of the subcontractors' previously demonstrated capability and performance. Audits are conducted to assure the effectiveness of the Mega Manufacturing supplier control system. For additional details, see *System* Procedure #40.61.

Clauses 4.6.3 through 4.8 are left out because no revision regarding ISO 14001 is required.

(4.9) Process Control

Mega Manufacturing has implemented and maintains production plans that directly affect quality *and environmental impacts* and ensures that these processes are carried out under controlled conditions. These plans include, but are not limited to, documented work instructions defining the manner of production, tooling to be used, environment, compliance with referenced standards/codes, *regulatory compliance,* and quality *and environmental management* plans. The system includes monitoring and control of suitable processes and product characteristics during production *and key characteristics of operations and activities that can have a significant impact on the environment and periodic evaluation of regulatory compliance.* The system also incorporates approval of processes, process operators, and equipment as required. The quality plan includes written criteria for workmanship standards. The Mega Manufacturing Training Manager maintains records to assure all special process operators are qualified or certified as required by specifications. The Production Manager of the Support Shops maintains records of special process equipment to ensure its continuing process capability. For additional details, see *System* Procedures #40.90, #40.91, #40.92, #40.93, #40.94, #40.95, and #40.96.

Clause 4.10 is left out because no revision regarding ISO 14001 is required.

(4.11) Control of Inspection, Measuring, and Test Equipment

(4.11.1) General

Mega Manufacturing maintains a calibration laboratory as a function of quality assurance. The calibration laboratory developed, implemented, and maintains a plan which assures all measurement and test equipment, including test software *used to fulfill requirements imposed by ISO 9002 and ISO 14001,* is controlled by the plan for both company-owned and personal tools. The *plan* identifies the measurements to be made and where they are to be made in the process. The plan requires records be generated and maintained that identify all calibrations, adjustments, and repairs made on measurement and test equipment. Equipment shall be used in a manner which ensures that measurement uncertainty is known and is consistent with the required measurement capability. The procedure provides provisions for the customer to confirm measuring and/or test results related to engines, modules, and parts they have contracted to have repaired *and customers and environmental regulatory agencies to confirm measuring and/or test results related to significant environmental impacts.*

(4.11.2) Control Procedure

1. All required measurements are specified by Engineering via the quality plan for the engine, module, and/or part *or by Operations for operations and activities with significant environmental impacts.* The inspector or mechanic will select the correct measuring and test equipment from the published document "Accuracy Use Limits for Standard Measuring Instruments."

2. The plan requires records be generated and maintained that identify all calibrations, adjustments, and repairs made on measurement and test equipment were performed in accordance with the National Institute of Standards and Technology and/or documented Mega Manufacturing standards.

3. Mega Manufacturing documented calibration procedures define the methods, equipment, frequency, acceptance criteria, and action to be taken.

4. The individual who performed the calibration will be identified on the record, and the date the next calibration is due will be identified on the measuring equipment.

5. The plan requires the Manager of Quality Control be notified when inspection, measuring, and test equipment is found to be out of calibration.

6. The procedure specifies the environmental conditions suitable to perform calibration and specifies handling, preservation, and storage instruction of inspection and test equipment. Measuring and test equipment will be stored in suitable containers to protect it from adverse conditions that could affect the accuracy of the equipment.
7. If measuring and test equipment is tampered with, dropped, or damaged, it is immediately returned to the Calibration Laboratory for the appropriate action. For additional details, see *System* Procedure #40.110.

Clauses 4.12 and 4.13 are left out because no revision regarding ISO 14001 is required.

(4.14) Corrective and Preventive Action

(4.14.1) General

Mega Manufacturing has implemented and maintains a procedure to assure that adequate investigation and corrective and preventive action is taken to eliminate the cause of nonconformances. As part of the investigation, controls are in place to assure the effectiveness of the corrective and preventive action.

(4.14.2) Corrective Action

Mega Manufacturing procedures apply to all nonconformances identified from internal/external *integrated-system* audits, customer complaints, employee-discovered discrepancies and chargeable test cell rejects. The procedures require analyzing processes, work operations, *records* and customer complaints to detect and eliminate causes of nonconformances. Corrective actions taken to eliminate the nonconformance are documented in the Nonconformance Database Log.

(4.14.3) Preventive Action

Mega Manufacturing procedures apply to all nonconformances identified from internal/external *integrated-system* audits, customer complaints, employee-discovered discrepancies, and chargeable test cell rejects. The procedures require analyzing processes, work operations, *records,* and customer complaints to detect and eliminate causes of nonconformances. Actions are taken to insure that a preventive action program is established to eliminate the potential causes of non-conformance documented in the Nonconformance Database Log. The Vice President of Quality Assurance will review all open corrective/preventive actions with the Executive Quality Committee on at least a quarterly basis. During this review, if any follow-up is required it will be assigned to the Mega Manufacturing ISO Audit Team. For additional details, see *System* Procedure #40.140.

Clause 4.15 is left out because no revision regarding ISO 14001 is required.

## (4.16) Control of *Records*

Mega Manufacturing has implemented and maintains a procedure that specifies the method of collecting, indexing, accessing, filing, storing, maintaining, and dispositioning all quality *and environmental management* records. Mega Manufacturing shop processing and subcontractors' records are audited to assure they are legible and complete before being stored in a suitable environment to minimize deterioration or damage. The records shall be stored and maintained in such a way that they can be readily retrieved. Where agreed contractually, quality *and environmental management* records shall be made available for evaluation by the customer or his representative. Records' retention times are established by contract with the customer, *by regulation, or by the designated management representative.* For additional details, see *System* Procedure #40.160.

## (4.17) Internal *System* Audits

Mega Manufacturing has implemented and maintains a system of internal *system* audits in accordance with the established procedures to verify the effectiveness of the *integrated* quality-*environmental management* system. The Vice President of Quality Assurance is responsible for establishing an audit schedule according to the importance of the activity being audited, assigning the auditors, and ensuring that follow-up actions are appropriate. All audits are documented and brought to the attention of the management personnel responsible for the area audited. The management personnel are responsible for taking timely corrective action on the deficiencies found by the audit. The Vice President of Quality Assurance will review all open audits with the Quality Executive Committee on at least a quarterly basis. For additional details, see *System* Procedures #40.170 and #40.171.

(4.18) Training

Mega Manufacturing has implemented and maintains procedures that identify the training needs of all personnel performing activities affecting quality *or having significant environmental aspects.* Appropriate training is provided in a timely manner. Records are maintained on these employees to assure they are qualified to perform the required work. Those employees that are required by regulation to be periodically certified in their job performance are monitored, and records are maintained to show they have satisfied all certification requirements. For additional details, see *System* Procedure #40.180.

Clauses 4.19 and 4.20 and Appendix A are left out because no revision regarding ISO 14001 is required.

*(4.21) Communication*

*Mega Manufacturing has implemented and maintains procedures to assure that information about all facets of the management system, including environmental aspects and impacts, environmental regulatory requirements, customer specifications, and customer satisfaction is communicated to relevant individuals and departments within the company. The Vice President, Operations, or his designee, is responsible for communications related to environmental issues. The Vice President, Marketing & Sales, is responsible for communication related to customer issues. For additional details, see System Procedure #40.210.*

*Mega Manufacturing also has implemented and maintains procedures to assure that relevant communication from out customers, regulators, and other external interested parties is received and documented and responded to in a timely manner. For additional details, see System Procedure #40.211.*

*At this time, Mega Manufacturing does not communicate externally about its significant environmental aspects except as required by law or regulation. This position is reviewed annually in conjunction with the third quarterly management review of the integrated system. For additional details, see System Procedure #40.10.*

*(4.22) Emergency Preparedness and Response*

*Mega Manufacturing has established and maintains four emergency response plans—Spill Prevention Countermeasures and Control Plan (see System Procedure #40.220), Contingency Plan for Emergency Procedures (see System Procedure #40.221), Facility Evacuation Plan (see System Procedure #40.222), and Safety Plan (see System Procedure #40.223). All plans are reviewed at least annually.*

# APPENDIX A

## Mega Manufacturing Mission Statement

Mega Manufacturing will strive to become the premier truck diesel engine service center worldwide. We will accomplish this by providing:

- Our *customers* with the highest quality engine maintenance services and meeting our commitments with respect to specifications, turn time, and cost.
- Our *employees* with challenging work assignments, a respectable work environment, and an excellent compensation package.
- Our *shareholders* with a superior return on investment.

# APPENDIX B

## ISO 9002-ISO 14001 Index

| System Manual Sections | ISO 9002 | ISO 14001 |
|---|---|---|
| 0.0   Introduction | | |
| 0.1   Approvals | | |
| 1.0   Scope and Field of Application | | |
| 1.1   Scope | | |
| 1.1   Field of Application | | |
| 2.0   References | | |
| 3.0   Definitions/Acronyms | | |
| 4.0   Integrated Quality-Environmental Management System Requirements | 4 | 4 |
| 4.1   Management Responsibility | 4.1 | 4.4.1 |
| 4.1.1 Quality and Environmental Policies | 4.1.1 | 4.2 |
| 4.1.2 Organization | 4.1.2 | 4.4.1 |
| 4.1.3 Management Review | 4.1.3 | 4.6 |
| 4.2   Quality-Environmental Management System | 4.2 | – |
| 4.2.1 General | 4.2.1 | 4.1,4.4.4 |
| 4.2.2 System Level Procedures | 4.2.2 | – |
| 4.2.3 Planning | 4.2.3 | 4.3.1, 4.3.2 |
| | | 4.3.3, 4.3.4 |
| 4.3   Contract Review | 4.2 | |

| System Manual Sections | ISO 9002 | ISO 14001 |
|---|---|---|
| 4.4    Design Control | N/A | |
| 4.5    Document and Data Control | 4.5 | 4.4.5 |
| 4.6    Purchasing | 4.6 | 4.4.6c |
| 4.7    Control of Customer-Supplied Product | 4.7 | |
| 4.8    Product Identification and Traceability | 4.8 | |
| 4.9    Process Control | 4.9 | 4.4.6a, b<br>4.5.1 ¶s 1, 3 |
| 4.10   Inspection and Testing | 4.10 | |
| 4.11   Control of Inspection, Measuring, and Test Equipment | 4.11 | 4.5.1, ¶2 |
| 4.12   Inspection and Test Status | 4.12 | |
| 4.13   Control of Nonconforming Product | 4.13 | |
| 4.14   Corrective and Preventive Action | 4.14 | 4.5.2 |
| 4.15   Handling, Storage, Packaging, Preservation, and Delivery | 4.15 | |
| 4.16   Control of Records | 4.16 | 4.5.3 |
| 4.17   Internal System Audits | 4.17 | 4.5.4 |
| 4.18   Training | 4.18 | 4.4.2 |
| 4.19   Servicing | 4.19 | |
| 4.20   Statistical Techniques | 4.20 | |
| 4.21   Communication | | 4.4.3 |
| 4.22   Emergency Preparedness and Response | | 4.4.7 |

# INDEX

167